Betsy Byars

Twayne's United States Authors Series

Ruth K. MacDonald, Editor
Bay Path College

TUSAS 636

BETSY BYARS

Betsy Byars

Malcolm Usrey

Clemson University, Emeritus

Twayne Publishers • New York
An Imprint of Simon & Schuster Macmillan

Prentice Hall International
London Mexico City New Delhi Singapore Sydney Toronto

Twayne's United States Authors Series No. 636

Betsy Byars
Malcolm Usrey

Twayne Publishers
An Imprint of Simon & Schuster Macmillan
866 Third Avenue
New York, NY 10022

Library of Congress Cataloging-in-Publication Data
Usrey, Malcolm.
    Betsy Byars/Malcolm Usrey.
        p. cm.—(Twayne's United States authors series; TUSAS 636)
    Includes bibliographical references and index.
    ISBN 0-8057-4536-X (alk. paper)
    1. Byars, Betsy Cromer—Criticism and interpretation. 2. Children's stories,
American—History and criticism. I. Title. II. Series.
PS3552.Y37Z9 1995
813'.54—dc20   95-8466
                                                                                  CIP

The paper used in this publication meets the minimum requirements of American
National Standard for Information Sciences—Permanence of Paper for Printed Library
Materials. ANSI Z39.48-1984.∞ ™

10 9 8 7 6 5 4 3 2 1

Printed in the United States of America

In Memory of
Henry Burt and Mattie Cathey Usrey
John Waller and Margaret Craig Cummins
Louise and Billie Cooke

Contents

Preface

Betsy Cromer Byars is first and foremost a writer for children, although her earliest publications in the late 1950s and early 1960s were humorous contributions to the "Post Script" pages of the old *Saturday Evening Post* and short articles for *Woman's Day* and *Family Circle*. This study seeks to show Byars's relationship to children's literature of the past 25 to 30 years and to show why she is considered one of the outstanding writers of realistic fiction for children of the past three decades.

The major portion of this study is in Chapter 2, analyses of nine of her major novels, and in Chapter 3, analyses of her two major series—the five-volume *Blossom* series and the four-volume *Bingo Brown* series—two series that are as well written and as pleasant to read as Eleanor Estes's *Moffat* series and Elizabeth Enright's *Melendy* series of half a century ago. Chapter 4 contains essays on Byars's style and on her use of irony and satire. Chapter 5 is about her elderly characterizations, which she is especially effective in creating and which appear in a number of her books. Chapter 6 assesses the achievement of Byars as a writer for children.

From 1962 and to the end of 1993 Byars has published 41 books for young readers, from the early grades through junior high school. Lack of space prohibits my presenting all 41 of these stories. The nine books analyzed in Chapter 2 and the nine analyzed in Chapter 3 are among Byars's best realistic fiction, of which she is a master; they are also the most representative of her works in subject, style, techniques, characterization, plot, and similar matters. If Byars had written only these 18, her reputation as a writer of realistic fiction for children would be assured.

While this study does not contain analyses of the remainder of the 41 books in Byars's canon, many of them have been cited in one place or another for various reasons, usually to exemplify or to support a hypothesis or generalization.

Acknowledgments

I am indebted to many people for help with this study. I am indebted to Betsy Cromer Byars for the time she spent in interviews and for the telephone calls I have made during the course of this study with questions that she cordially and enthusiastically answered. I am indebted to her for her encouragement in lending me materials from her files, which have become a part of the Clemson University Libraries Special Collections. Above all, however, I am indebted to Byars for the many, many hours of pleasure I have had from reading and rereading her 41 books for children and for the pleasure that writing about her work has given me for the past few years. I am also in her debt for her gracious permission to quote from her works.

I am indebted to Delacorte Press of Bantam Doubleday Dell and to HarperCollins for their permission to quote from books each has published by Byars.

I am indebted to Viking Penguin for permission to quote from the following books:

After the Goat Man by Betsy Byars. Copyright © 1974 by Betsy Byars. Used by permission of Viking Penguin, a division of Penguin Books USA Inc.

Bingo Brown and the Language of Love by Betsy Byars. Copyright © 1989 by Betsy Byars. Used by permission of Viking Penguin, a division of Penguin Books USA Inc.

Bingo Brown, Gypsy Lover by Betsy Byars. Copyright © 1990 by Betsy Byars. Used by permission of Viking Penguin, a division of Penguin Books USA Inc.

Bingo Brown's Guide to Romance by Betsy Byars. Copyright © 1992 by Betsy Byars. Used by permission of Viking Penguin, a division of Penguin Books USA Inc.

The Burning Questions of Bingo Brown by Betsy Byars. Copyright © 1988 by Betsy Byars. Used by permission of Viking Penguin, a division of Penguin Books USA Inc.

The Cartoonist by Betsy Byars. Copyright © 1978 by Betsy Byars. Used by permission of Viking Penguin, a division of Penguin Books USA Inc.

Cracker Jackson by Betsy Byars. Copyright © 1985 by Betsy Byars. Used by permission of Viking Penguin, a division of Penguin Books USA Inc.

The 18th Emergency by Betsy Byars. Copyright © 1973 by Betsy Byars. Used by permission of Viking Penguin, a division of Penguin Books USA Inc.

The Glory Girl by Betsy Byars. Copyright © 1983 by Betsy Byars. Used by permission of Viking Penguin, a division of Penguin Books USA Inc.

The House of Wings by Betsy Byars. Copyright © 1972 by Betsy Byars. Used by permission of Viking Penguin, a division of Penguin Books USA Inc.

The Midnight Fox by Betsy Byars. Copyright © 1968 by Betsy Byars. Used by permission of Viking Penguin, a division of Penguin Books USA Inc.

McMummy by Betsy Byars. Copyright © 1993 by Betsy Byars. Used by permission of Viking Penguin, a division of Penguin Books USA Inc.

The Summer of the Swans by Betsy Byars. Copyright © 1970 by Betsy Byars. Used by permission of Viking Penguin, a division of Penguin Books USA Inc.

Trouble River by Betsy Byars, Puffin cover illustration by Lonnie Knabel. Copyright © 1989 by Lonnie Knabel for cover illustration. Used by permission of Puffin Books, a division of Penguin Books USA Inc.

I am indebted to two graduate students, Darlene O'Dell and Deanna Ramey, each of whom spent a summer helping me with this study.

I am indebted to several staff members of Clemson University's Robert Muldrow Cooper Library for their kind, patient help and support, particularly Marian Withington, humanities reference and interloan librarian. Marian has always been able to locate the obscurest information after the rest of us have given up. And I am indebted to Ida Foster, humanities reference librarian, for her help with various questions and concerns. I am indebted to Iris Maw, circulation librarian, for her help in keeping me supplied with copies of Byars's novels. I am indebted to Pat Scales, librarian at Greenville Middle School and adjunct professor of children's literature at Furman University, for discussing with me elderly characters in various writers' works.

I am indebted to hundreds of graduate and undergraduate students in my children's literature classes over the past 25 years whose enthusiasm for and appreciation of children's literature have deepened and enhanced my own, specifically for the work of children's illustrators and writers, including that of Byars.

And I am indebted to my wife, Katie, and to close friends, particularly Julie and Lynn Craig, who have gone beyond familial loyalty and friendship to listen enthusiastically and appreciatively to pages and pages of manuscript. I am also indebted to my friends and colleagues, Ned Willey, Harold Woodell, and Lucy Rollin, for their enthusiasm and encouragement for every study I have undertaken, including this one.

Chronology

1928	Betsy Alice Cromer Byars is born Tuesday, 7 August, in Charlotte, North Carolina, to George Guy and Nan Aline Rugheimer Cromer.
1935	Family moves to Hoskins Mill, near Charlotte.
1938	Family returns to Charlotte.
1946	Graduates from Central High School, Charlotte.
1946	Enrolls in Furman University, Greenville, South Carolina.
1948	Transfers to Queens College, Charlotte.
1950	Graduates with B.A. in English; marries Ed Ford Byars; moves to Clemson, South Carolina, where Ed is professor of engineering.
1951	Nancy Laura (Laurie) born.
1953	Betsy Ann born.
1956	Family moves to Urbana, Illinois; Nan Aline born.
1958	Guy Ford born; family returns to Clemson.
1960	Family moves to Morgantown, West Virginia.
1962	*Clementine.*
1965	*The Dancing Camel.*
1966	*Rama, the Gypsy Cat.*
1967	*The Groober.*
1968	*The Midnight Fox.*
1969	*Trouble River.*
1970	*The Summer of the Swans.*
1971	Awarded the Newbery Medal for *The Summer of the Swans. Go and Hush the Baby.*
1972	*The House of Wings.*
1973	*The Winged Colt of Casa Mia; The 18th Emergency.*
1974	*After the Goat Man.*

1975   *The Lace Snail.*

1976   *The TV Kid.*

1977   *The Pinballs.*

1978   *The Cartoonist.*

1979   *Good-bye, Chicken Little.*

1980   Family moves to Clemson. *The Night Swimmers.*

1981   Awarded the American Book Award for *The Night Swimmers. The Cybil War.*

1982   *The Animal, the Vegetable, and John D Jones; The Two-Thousand-Pound Goldfish.*

1983   *The Glory Girl.*

1984   *The Computer Nut.*

1985   *Cracker Jackson; The Golly Sisters Go West.*

1986   *The Not-Just-Anybody Family; The Blossoms Meet the Vulture Lady.*

1987   *The Blossoms and the Green Phantom; A Blossom Promise.*

1988   *The Burning Questions of Bingo Brown; Beans on the Roof.*

1989   *Bingo Brown and the Language of Love.*

1990   *Bingo Brown, Gypsy Lover; Hooray for the Golly Sisters!*

1991   *The Seven Treasure Hunts; Wanted . . . Mud Blossom; The Moon and I.*

1992   *Bingo Brown's Guide to Romance; Coast to Coast.*

1993   *McMummy.*

Chapter One

Goats, Coffins, Planes, Typewriters, and Snakes

Background, experiences, people, talent, imagination, ambition, determination, hard work, and "good scraps" make a writer of fiction. Pens, pencils, paper, and a typewriter help, too. "Good scraps" are things that Betsy Cromer Byars sees, reads, and hears and works into her stories at appropriate places.[1]

Family and Background

At first glance, Betsy Byars's background and experiences and the people in her life might not indicate that she would ever become a writer. She was born on Tuesday, 7 August 1928, in Charlotte, North Carolina. Her sister, Nancy, was two and a half years older. Byars's family lived in a bungalow at 915 Magnolia Avenue in Charlotte until they moved in 1935 to Hoskins Mill, north of Charlotte, where Byars's father worked as a bookkeeper. Hoskins Mill, near Mt. Holly, no longer exists; it was bulldozed for an interstate highway many years ago. The family returned to Charlotte in 1938, back to Magnolia Avenue where they remained until about the time Byars was graduated from college in 1950.[2]

Some of the people who make up Byars's background and experiences begin with her maternal and paternal grandparents. Her mother's people were Rugheimers of Charleston; her grandfather Rugheimer, a second-generation German immigrant, had a business tailoring uniforms for the cadets at the Citadel, until recently, one of two all-male military schools in the United States. Grandma in *The Two-Thousand-Pound Goldfish* (1982) is a collector of pillows, perfume bottles, and miniature lamps, but Grandfather Rugheimer's collections were somewhat rarer, "rare coins, rare stamps, rare books, and rare tropical fish," none of which Betsy and and her sister, Nancy, were allowed to touch, though on occasion Betsy did touch them in secret. One of Grandfather Rugheimer's rare books was a collection of Bible stories illustrated with dark and somber pictures—"The Jews Descending into the Fiery Furnace," "Gabriel Wrestling with the Angel of Death"—and one of Noah's Ark floating in the background and in the foreground, a mountaintop depicting "desperate people and animals" struggling to survive.[3] These pictures bothered Betsy for some time because their content would disturb a child, but perhaps, too, because she was partaking of forbidden fruits. Byars describes her grandmother Rugheimer as "elegant," well dressed with "jewelry—lots of jewelry" (Int).

Byars's mother, Nan Aline, was somewhat like her own mother, a pretty woman who fell in love with and married Byars's father, George Guy Cromer, in the early to mid-1920s when he was working his way through the Citadel after World War I. Mr. Cromer's background, however, was different from that of the Rugheimers in Charleston, the principal city of the "low-country" of South Carolina. Mr. Cromer was from the Anderson area of the "up-country," the Piedmont of the Blue Ridge Mountains. Low-country people were heirs to a culture going back to a time when Charleston was one of the cultural centers of the colonies and the early United States. Up-country people were heirs to a less-cultured, largely rural life made up of large plantations that were far out-numbered by smallholdings of yeomen farmers who worked the land themselves. Byars describes her Cromer ancestors as down-to-earth people, "in the best sense of the word, country people." They were plain people; her grandmother could shoot a gun as well as any man, and she made her own dresses, always of one style and from "very plain gingham" (Int).

Though she has never said so, some of the elderly women characters in her canon may have been at least partly drawn from her two grandmothers. Perhaps there is something of her Grandmother Cromer in Mad Mary of the *Blossom* series, and perhaps there is something of her Grandmother Rugheimer and her mother in Grammy in the *Bingo Brown* series. And there is perhaps something of her Cromer grandfather or some of the male members of his family—those good country people—incorporated into one or two of the elderly male characters such as Sammy's grandfather in *The House of Wings* (1972) or Ira Gryshevich in *After the Goat Man* (1974) or Pap in the *Blossom* series. For sure, there is something of her Grandfather Cromer in *The Pinballs* (1977), one of Byars's "good scraps." When she was small, Grandfather Cromer took Byars with him to pay his respects to Uncle Joe, lying in the parlor at his home in a homemade coffin, which Byars accidentally kicked as her grandfather picked her up to look at Uncle Joe. To Byars's consternation, her accidentally kicking the coffin caused Uncle Joe's mouth to fall open, revealing a mouth stuffed with rags. She used this incident in *The Pinballs* when Mr. Mason, the foster parent, tells Thomas J about the time when he was a child and accidentally kicked a coffin, causing a dead man's mouth to fall open (*Moon*, 41–42).

Byars's father, Guy Cromer, may have influenced her writing in a somewhat unexpected way. He was not only a hard-working man, but a determined one, too. Though he was trained as an engineer, he took a job as a bookkeeper in the Hoskins Mill, because jobs were hard to get and keep. Though Hoskins changed hands and merged during his tenure with the mill, Mr. Cromer's determination paid off. He eventually became treasurer of the company; he was transferred to New York for a time, and afterwards returned to live and work in Anderson until he retired. Perhaps Byars inherited her father's sense of determination. During the early days of her writing career, Byars had many rejection slips for her work, and even though they kept coming, she worked hard and never lost her determination to become a published writer (Int).

Byars has a great sense of humor. It takes no great effort to realize she does after reading a few of her novels. At parties and other social functions, her sense of humor is infectious, and whomever she talks with is soon laughing at some anecdote or story she tells; and she is just as quick to see and respond to funny stories that others tell her, her laughter ringing out across a room, causing other guests to wish they were talking with Byars.

Byars says that she inherited her sense of humor from her parents, her Grandmother Rugheimer, and her Rugheimer aunts and uncle. At family gatherings they regaled one another with oft-repeated family stories, and they laughed every time they heard the stories, no matter how often they heard them (Int). Although Guy Cromer was a hardworking and sometimes stern man, he was also fun-loving, as Byars indicates in relating how he read "Goldilocks and the Three Bears" to her when she was a child. Instead of saying that someone had been eating his porridge, her father would read, "Somebody's been eating my corn flakes" and "Somebody's been sleeping on my Beauty Rest mattress" (*Author*, 54). Byars has Cracker Jackson's father read the story to Cracker with similar changes, though brought up to date. Instead of corn flakes, Cracker's father reads "low-fat yogurt" and "Serta Perfect-Sleeper."[4]

Although Byars has not said that the Cromers were storytellers, they likely were, too. Those family stories, repeated as often as they were, probably became as honed and polished as the old folk tales, handed down from generation to generation with their punch lines well timed.

If Byars were influenced by the method of these oral stories and by the stories themselves, she is little different from other writers who absorbed something about the art of storytelling from their families. A number of southern writers have claimed that they learned aspects of the art of story-telling from their families—writers such as Robert Burch, whose stories are well laced with humorous and delightful southerners and well-timed anecdotes. Hearing her relatives' stories probably helped in Byars's ability to re-create the rhythm and idiom of dialogue (*Moon*, 32).

Childhood, Schools, and Marriage

In *The Green and Burning Tree* Eleanor Cameron points out that many of the writers of English fantasies had unhappy, lonely childhoods and theorizes that their unhappy childhoods may have had a part in their creating "vivid inner live[s]," which in turn helped them to write good fantasies.[5] Perhaps the corollary of Cameron's hypothesis is that a happy childhood may have a part in writers' creating good and humorous realism. Like all children, Byars probably escaped into a fantasy world of her own creation occasionally, but not with the intensity that writers such as Hans Christian Andersen and Beatrix Potter did as children. Byars's childhood, by comparison, was entirely normal, and she was much too involved in play and school and social activities to have been forced very long into an inner life of her own creation.

Even so, like many children and adults, Byars may have used reading as a means of escape. She learned to read when she was four years old, unintentionally taught by her sister, Nancy, when they frequently played school. When she and Nancy were still children, Nancy took her to the public library in Charlotte and showed her the shelves of "good books"—long, long romance novels, which Byars did not stop reading until she had read all of them on the shelves. She did not discover until she was an adult and a published children's author herself that the Charlotte library had a children's room in an annex. Thus Byars became early in life an avid, life-long reader, and reading has been a significant influence on her writing. One of the things she had to give up when she and her husband, Ed Byars, moved to Clemson from Morgantown in 1980 was her personal library—mostly contemporary novels for adults and some for children—which she sold at a huge yard and garage sale in Morgantown because their Clemson townhouse did not have room for her books. With Ed's encouragement and sympathy, she sold all her books from a shelf-lined room, and later, when Ed retired from Clemson

University and brought home boxes and boxes of books, she discovered he had not given up his personal library, having had it shipped to his office on the campus. With her usual good humor, Betsy accepted Ed's ruse to keep his library (Int).

Byars is often asked if she reads children's fiction written by other writers. She says she does, but perhaps not with the ardor she reads adult fiction. What she does try to read of children's writers' books are those titles that children in her visits to schools mention over and over because she wants to know what children like and are reading.[6]

School is also a part of Byars's life and background—both the schools of her childhood and schools of today. The latter she is more familiar with and more knowledgeable about because of her visits to schools and because her four children often shared their school experiences with her. "I could have never written for young people if I had not had kids. My kids were very communicative. They would come home from school saying, "Guess what happened today?" or, "Here's what happened to me" (Mazurkiewicz and Ross, 72). Some of her protagonists and other characters in her stories are in school or they relate incidents about school. School is an important part of Bingo Brown's life in the series about him, and school is important to the Bean children, particularly to Anna, in *Beans on the Roof* (1988).

Byars remembers many things about her own school years, particularly, her first grade teacher at Dilworth Elementary in Charlotte. When Nancy started to school in Charlotte about 1932, her first-grade teacher was Miss Harriet, who practiced delightful and entertaining teaching and learning, including having a store made out of orange crates with products for sale in the form of empty boxes and cans and the like that the children brought from home. The children had play money; they bought, sold, and made change, enhancing their skills in arithmetic. From the moment she heard Nancy tell about Miss Harriet's store, Betsy wanted to go to school, and above all else to be in Miss Harriet's room. After an interminable two or three years' wait, Betsy was old enough to start school. When the students' names were called out to go with Miss Harriet, Betsy's name was not among them. She arose from her seat and followed Miss Harriet and the children to Miss Harriet's room. The teacher whom Betsy had been assigned missed her and reported the "lost" child to the principal, who took Nancy with her from room to room to locate Betsy, as only Nancy could recognize her. Coming to Miss Harriet's room with the principal, Miss Blankenship, Nancy pointed out Betsy. Miss Blankenship said she would take her to her assigned teacher and room so Betsy would not get lost again. Not looking at Miss Blankenship, but directly at the top of her desk, Betsy said, "I want to be in Miss Harriet's room." No one said anything. Dead silence. Still looking at the top of her desk, she changed her statement to, "I have to be in Miss Harriet's room." Miss Harriet said, "Let her stay"; Miss Blankenship hesitated while "the world ground to a halt." Then, Miss Harriet said more firmly, "Yes, let her stay." The world began to move again "with an audible click" (Int and *Moon*, 71–72).

Byars's choice of college to attend was made for a similar reason: Furman University looked like fun. Sometime during 1946, Byars and her mother drove to Anderson to visit the Cromer grandparents; accompanying them was the daughter of one of Mrs. Cromer's friends, whom they delivered to the old Furman University campus near downtown Greenville. Seeing all the young men on the campus, Byars decided then and there that Furman was the college for her. She did not learn until she enrolled that fall that they had delivered the friend to the boys' campus, not the girls', separated from each other by about a mile. At Furman, Byars planned to major in math, but calculus proved to be more of a challenge than she wanted—not that she was a poor student, just not interested in math. Majoring in math was inspired by Nancy's being a math major, and the idea of "sister mathematicians" had a nice romantic appeal to it, especially in those days when few girls majored in math. Furman was a strict school, and Byars often found herself on probation for some minor infractions. As a result of the strictures and her not liking calculus, Byars changed her major to English and transferred to Queens College in Charlotte between her sophomore and junior years. Why she chose Queens is not certain, but it was not because of the young men at Queens; it did not become co-educational until 1987.

In the summer of 1949 Byars met a person who would be an important part of her life and would be another influence, directly and indirectly, on her writing. Needing a course that she could not get at Queens, she enrolled in Winthrop College in Rock Hill, South Carolina, and met Ed Ford Byars, a young college professor from Clemson University, at home with his parents in Rock Hill that summer selling cutlery door to door. Clemson employed only senior professors during summer school. Ed was tall, handsome, had a Mercury convertible, and an antique 1931 Stinson plane. Ed and Betsy were married on 24 June 1950, in Anderson, South Carolina, where her parents had recently moved. In those days air-conditioning was nearly as rare as California condors, and their hands swelled so much in the heat that they could hardly get their rings on each other's fin-

gers. Betsy and Ed began their life together in one of the old metal build-
ings, surplus military housing, brought to the Clemson campus after
World War II, known as "prefabs." Later, they moved to the new, recently
built faculty housing in Douthit Hills above the Clemson campus. While
they were living there they designed and built a house on Poole Lane,
which they owned until they left Clemson for West Virginia in 1960.

Two of their children, Betsy Ann and Laurie, were born while they
were living in Clemson and before Ed returned to graduate school at the
University of Illinois in Urbana in 1956. Nan Aline was born in 1956,
and Guy Ford was born in 1958 in Urbana. As they were growing up,
the children and their friends added a new and important part to Byars's
experiences, many incorporated into her fiction. During those years the
children sometimes served as reader-critics. She might ask one of them
to read a manuscript until he or she lost interest; at times, a manuscript
did not always hold their interest for long. Guy read the manuscript of
After the Goat Man and told his mother that if he'd known it was to end
the way it did, he would not have read it. She revised the ending, and
she thinks she made the book better (Mazurkiewicz and Ross, 74).

Byars's Writing Career

Although Byars was an English major and loved reading, she had
never thought about becoming a writer until after she and Ed moved to
Urbana so that Ed could finish his Ph.D. She had never had a desire to
become a professional writer even though all through school writing had
always been easy for her—themes, essays, term papers came readily.
Byars began submitting short humorous pieces to the "Post Scripts"
page editor at the *Saturday Evening Post*, and she received $75 for each
piece the periodical published. What prompted her to try to write was
the reason that many women go to work—for extra money (Int). There
was, however, more than money; Byars was ambitious and became
determined to write more than for the "Post Scripts" page.

While still in Illinois, Byars discovered children's books. One of the
highlights of the week was the bookmobile's visit to the barracks apartments. Byars and her two daughters, Laurie and Betsy Ann, then about
five and seven, took as many books as allowed from the bookmobile.
Sharing some of the children's books with Laurie and Betsy, Byars began
to wonder how a few of the books could ever have found publishers. Some
of the books seemed unbelievably ridiculous; one in particular—a book
with no plot and simple, short repeated sentences—made Byars wonder

how publishers could pay people to write such books. This and other books she shared with her daughters planted a seed in Byars's mind. She began to think about writing books for children, and after a time she began writing books for children. Rejections came about as fast as Byars sent out manuscripts (Int). Byars says, "One of the reasons I started writing children's books was that I thought they would be so easy—they just seemed like nothing to me. The harder I tried to write one, the more interested I became. Finally, maybe ten years after I began to write, that was all I was concentrating on" (Mazurkiewicz and Ross, 72).

By the time the Byarses returned to Clemson in June of 1958, their son, Guy Ford, was about two months old, and Byars was publishing articles in *Woman's Day* and *Family Circle*. Not having any success with her children's stories, her ambition and determination increasing, and wanting to branch out, to find other genres, she began writing mysteries. An ardent fan of mysteries, Betsy thought she should be able to write them. Ed would start reading them, and by the time he had read two pages, he would say, "Jim Bose did it." Byars gave up writing mysteries, although her most recent book, *The Dark Stairs* (1994), is a mystery for children.

In the summer of 1959 Ed was working on a project in his laboratory on the Clemson campus one Saturday morning when the new dean of engineering of the University of West Virginia, on his way to Florida, stopped to see Clemson's fairly new engineering building. Ed showed him around, and they had a good visit. Later that fall the dean wrote Ed asking him to become the head of the mechanical engineering department at the University of West Virginia with twice the salary he was making. After a visit to Morgantown to see the city and the University and to meet the faculty, Ed took the job. The Byarses moved in January 1960. They lived in a rented house until it sold, then moved to another house while constructing the house at 641 Vista Place, where they would live during the rest of their time in Morgantown. It was a two-story house with four or five bedrooms and a large basement and attic.

In Morgantown, Byars again began working on writing children's stories. She had written five self-contained episodes about a dragon, which other publishers had rejected until she sent it to Houghton Mifflin. In a letter the editor expressed interest in the stories, though one of them the editor did not like, adding that she needed seven stories. That night, Byars sat down and wrote three more stories and sent them in. Months passed, and Byars wrote asking for news about them. The editor replied that she was looking for an illustrator for the stories. More months passed, and then one day, Byars went to the mailbox and found a package (Int). It was cold, and it was snowing. Byars was wearing a sweater, and she was cold. All she wanted to do was get the mail and get back into the house. As soon as she saw the package, she knew it was *Clementine* (1962). Standing by the mailbox at the end of the drive, she tore open the package. "It was a moment of absolute magic. . . . It was if I had gotten an idea for a book that morning, come to the mailbox, and—presto—here it was. It was completely, absolutely, unforgettably—magic" (*Author*, 62).

Byars sent a manuscript to Viking, where Annis Duff, among the best and most experienced children's book editors of the time, became her editor. Duff was the first of several fine editors who helped Byars with her writing. She submitted the manuscript for *Trouble River*, but it was not published until 1969, a year after *The Midnight Fox* was published, although *Trouble River* had been written first. When Duff first received the manuscript for *Trouble River* she told Byars she did not think it a publishable book. It was only with Duff's "patient help and keen insight that it turned out to be a publishable book after all" (*Author*, 62).

Although she may not have realized it at the time, with *The Midnight Fox*, one of her best books, Byars found her metier: contemporary realism for children. While there are some good qualities about *Trouble River*, historical realism, it is not among Byars's best novels. Its plot is well-paced; cranky, decrepit, and grumbling, Grandma is more flat than round; and Dewey is the first of a long line of skillfully drawn boy characters. The story, however, has its flaws. It is improbable that a pregnant pioneer mother would leave her home to have her baby; Dewey's father has turned all his pigs loose except two boars, which he's fattening for butchering. Meat from boars gives off a terrible odor while it is cooking, and it is unpalatable and all but inedible, something any American pioneer would have known.[7] It seems a little beyond plausibility that Dewey, Grandma in a rocking chair, and a dog could get down Trouble River on a raft six by eight feet wide without getting more than a little wet. Byars, of course, realized that getting the three and the raft down the river and over stiff falls without a tumble into the water is unrealistic, but as is often the case with a character, Grandma got the upper hand and would not let Byars dump her into the river.[8]

The Midnight Fox and *The Summer of the Swans* (1970) were turning points in Byars's career. Since she wrote these two novels she has gone on to write and publish at least two dozen realistic stories that make her one of the leading writers of realistic fiction for children in the United States and in other countries, particularly in England, where she is widely read.

Another part of Byars's life she has used in her writing is animals. At Hoskins one of her first pets was a goat named Buttsy (*Moon*, 12). Dogs and other animals appear frequently in her stories, though dogs win by a wide margin, obviously her favorite animal. There are all kinds of dogs in her life and in her stories. She has proved to be a keen observer of animals, often doing wide-ranging research on a specific animal, capturing the essence of the animal she is writing about as she does in *The House of Wings* (1972). In the *Blossom* series she devotes a lot of attention to two dogs, Mud and Dump. The last book in the series is *Wanted . . . Mud Blossom* (1991), dedicated to 11 dogs.

Among her most recent pets have been snakes. Moon is a wild black snake she found on the porch of their log house outside of Clemson where Byars spent her days writing as long as she and Ed owned the house. Moon was not a pet in the usual sense of the word (it stayed outside) but an animal Byars favored and read about in the library and that she relates her encounters with in her memoir, *The Moon and I* (1991). She also relates in the book how she came to buy Freckles, a speckled king snake, which she keeps in a cage. It has escaped at least twice, revealing that it is an escape artist. Though she thinks one book about a snake is enough, she cannot resist typing a possible title for another book (titles are sometimes the starting point for a story), "A Snake Named Freckles" (*Moon*, 92–94).

In 1980 Betsy and Ed moved back to Clemson where Ed had been appointed special assistant to Bill Atchley, president of Clemson University. They bought a townhouse on Lake Hartwell and later bought a log house near Oconee County Airport to be near their planes and as a place for Betsy to write while Ed worked at restoring and rebuilding antique airplanes at the airport after he retired in May 1985. In 1992 they sold the log house and built a house with a hangar near a private landing strip, where Betsy does her writing on a computer.

All four of Ed and Betsy's children were graduated from Clemson University. Betsy Ann Duffey lives in Atlanta and has published several books for children; Laurie Meyers has published two books for children; under her maiden name, Nan Boekelheide is a professor of engineering in Charlotte, North Carolina; and Guy Ford works for a computer firm in Cincinnatti, his skill with computers attested to by his computer-made illustrations for Byars's *The Computer Nut* (1984).

When Byars began writing, she had two talents: her "ease with words (which came from a lifelong habit of reading)" and her "ease with dialogue (which came from being born into a family of talkers)." Everything else she had to learn the hard way, she says (*Moon, 32*). Byars also knew how to type, and typewriters have played a role in Byars's writing career, although they have not had the same kind of influence on her writing as people and dogs and snakes have had. Her first typewriter was an old one, so old that the *i* stuck, all the insides of letters like *a, e,* and *o* were clogged with dried ink, and the *t* always printed higher than the other letters (Mazurkiewicz and Ross, 38). In the barracks apartment in Illinois, the typewriter sat at Byars's place at the dining table, which she pushed aside when she ate (Int). Eventually she graduated to an electric typewriter, then to an electronic typewriter, which could erase mistakes. About 1982 she began using a computer and wrote *The Glory Girl* (1983) with it (*Author*, 67).

In their home in Morgantown, Betsy wrote in her and Ed's bedroom at a large, L-shaped desk under a window looking out over the West Virginia hills. In the townhouse in Clemson, she wrote for a little while at the kitchen table, but later moved to a small desk in an upstairs room with a view of Lake Hartwell. Ed and Betsy continue to live in the townhouse on Lake Hartwell. When they bought the log house near the airport, Byars spent her writing days there until they sold it and built their hangar house. She writes there on a Macintosh computer in an upstairs room by a north window looking out over the hills of South Carolina. The wall above her desk is decorated with a number of framed pictures depicting characters, scenes, and incidents from her books.

In one sense there is a great distance from 915 Magnolia Avenue in Charlotte, North Carolina, to a hangar house near Clemson, South Carolina; in another sense, however, the distance is not great because in between there is a continuity of people, experiences, animals, talent, ambition, determination, and lots of "good scraps" that have made Betsy Byars one of the major writers of realistic fiction for children of the past 25 years, a writer whose books are read and loved by millions.

Chapter Two

The Major Novels

The novels discussed in this chapter have much in common; each deals with young protagonists who have conflicts, ranging from parental desertion and a painful relationship with a grandparent in *The House of Wings* and in *The Two-Thousand-Pound Goldfish* to child and wife abuse in *Cracker Jackson*.

Sometimes the conflict is a personal one, what critics often call "person against self," exhibited in *The Midnight Fox* when Tom has to spend a couple of months on the farm with friends of his parents while they vacation in Europe. Tom does not want to go to the farm, but after a few days he makes a discovery that changes his feelings about being there. The discovery brings about changes in Tom, and he finds there an inner strength he did not know he possessed. Sara, the protagonist of *The Summer of the Swans*, has a similar conflict. She is dissatisfied with the way she looks, but when her retarded brother wanders away from their house and becomes lost one night, Sara also learns an important truth about herself and about life.

The conflicts the three children in *The Pinballs* face are not those that can be easily overcome. Two of the children, Carlie and Harvey have suffered emotional and physical abuse from their parents. Thomas J's parents abandoned him when he was a baby. The emotional scars left from these conflicts are not resolved in the story, although more immediate ones are. Byars plays down this larger conflict of emotional scars, and by concentrating on their immediate problems she gives the novel a satisfying ending.

The protagonists of these stories also have in common inner strengths that help to lessen, resolve, or overcome their problems and conflicts. Adults often give guidance, but the resolutions usually stem from discoveries or epiphanies of the protagonists themselves. These boys and girls are not unlike folk-tale heroes who endured all kinds of hardships and conflicts in their lives and who overcame almost insurmountable obstacles.

Another thing these young protagonists have in common is that with the exception of Harold V. Coleman in *After the Goat Man*, either one or both parents are not present. There are various reasons for one or both parents to be missing: the parents are vacationing, in hiding, divorced, or dead. The children live with a grandparent, another relative, friends, a single parent, or with foster parents.

These stories represent Byars's best fiction. They deal with young protagonists courageously and resolutely working out their conflicts. The protagonists and the supporting characters, both old and young, are among the most memorable characterizations in realistic fiction of the past 25 years.

The Midnight Fox

The Midnight Fox (1968), Byars's fifth published story, opens when Tom, the nine-year-old protagonist, learns from his mother that he is to spend a couple of months with Aunt Millie and Uncle Fred on their farm while Tom's mother and father bicycle in Europe with friends. Afraid he will be bored on the farm and will miss working on his models and will miss his friend Petie Burkis, Tom says he does not want to go. Little his mother or father says can change his mind, although Tom sarcastically agrees to his father's wish to put up a good front for his mother's sake.

Tom feels somewhat abandoned when his parents leave him with Uncle Fred, Aunt Millie, and their overweight daughter, Hazeline. Aunt Millie shows him to his room, her son Bubba's old room, a typical boy's room with its shotgun, stuffed squirrel, and birds' eggs and nests. Out one of the windows, Aunt Millie points to a tree that her sons had climbed up and down without a thought but that Tom knows he will never use as a means of getting in and out of the room because he is not adventurous.

Tom's first three days at the farm are long and tedious; going for the mail each day is the only respite from his boredom and unhappiness. On the third or fourth day, a letter from Petie takes him over to a pasture where he sits to write Petie. Just as Tom finishes his letter, he sees for the first time the black fox. Tom is so excited about seeing the fox that he wishes he could "see . . . the fox leaping over the grass again. In all my life I have never been so excited."[1] This first and subsequent sightings of the fox change Tom's outlook about the farm and about his aunt and uncle. Tom is so captivated by the beauty and grace of the fox that he spends his days looking for and learning about the fox by observing her and by asking Hazeline and Uncle Fred questions about foxes.

The beauty and grace of the vixen and Tom's sightings of her become the center of his life, and he spends hours silently, quietly watching for her. In the following weeks he sees the fox 15 times, making a notch on his suitcase for each sighting. He does not tell anyone he has seen her. One day, when Tom comes close to her den, she leads him away from it; another time he accidentally finds her den and sees her bring a bird to her cub and delights in the cub's play with it.

But Tom's pleasure turns to concern when the black fox begins to raid Aunt Millie's poultry. At Aunt Millie's insistence, Uncle Fred finds the den, takes the young fox, and locks it in an empty rabbit hutch to lure the vixen into shooting range.

Just about dark, the vixen comes to rescue the young fox, and Uncle Fred shoots and misses because a noise distracts him. A summer thunderstorm hits, driving everyone inside, and Uncle Fred says he will get the vixen the next night. Although Tom knows that the fox is destructive, that Aunt Millie and Uncle Fred will be disappointed in him, and that he will have to climb down the tree to let the young fox loose, he faces his doubts and fears, and slowly and anxiously climbs down the tree in the storm to let the young fox out of the cage. Because he cannot climb back up the tree and because he realizes that Aunt Millie and Uncle Fred will soon learn that the young fox has been freed, Tom simply rings the front door bell and confesses; neither Aunt Millie nor Uncle Fred is upset by his confession. They say little and never tell his parents about his letting the young fox out. Uncle Fred admits to Tom that he "never like to see wild things in a pen myself" (*Fox*, 147). A few days later, Tom's parents come for him, and he leaves the farm.

Like many realistic stories for young readers, *The Midnight Fox* is a bildungsroman, a story in which the protagonist grows and matures, makes an important discovery leading to a change, usually for the better. As Tom and his parents leave the farm, Tom wants "to say the greatest thing in the world to Aunt Millie and Uncle Fred because I had realized after I let the fox go that they were probably the nicest people I would ever meet. In all the past week they had never mentioned once what I had done" (*Fox*, 155). Tom's realization about Aunt Millie and Uncle Fred stems from a change within himself; Aunt Millie and Uncle Fred have not changed.

Tom's greater maturity is also evident in his recognition that a world exists beyond the models with which he has filled his room at home. Returning home, Tom sees that everything is just the same as when he left, everything except his room: "The only thing that seemed the least bit different to me was when I went in my room, because all I could see at first was models, hundreds of models everywhere. You would have thought that I had done nothing all my life but glue pieces of plastic together. That was funny, too, because when I was at the farm remembering my room, I had never thought once about all these models" (*Fox*, 156).

Tom has also discovered natural beauty in the farm and in the vixen. Even after five years when he relates the story of his summer, it is his first sighting of the fox in her natural environment that he remembers most vividly. "Sometimes at night when the rain is beating against the windows of my room, I think about that summer on the farm. It has been five years, but when I close my eyes I am once again by the creek watching the black fox come leaping over the green, green grass. She is light and free as the wind, exactly as she was the first time I saw her" (*Fox*, 9).

And despite Tom's lack of courage throughout most of the novel, his courage in freeing the baby fox and his courage in accepting the consequences of his act by facing Aunt Millie and Uncle Fred with his deed immediately after freeing the fox indicate a step, if not a leap, toward maturity.

Tom's increased maturity is also evident at the end of the novel as he recalls his summer at the farm: "It was if it had happened to another boy, not me at all." From his statement Tom would seem to have gained little or nothing from the experience, to have not been affected by it. That he remembers most vividly the night he let the baby fox out indicates he realizes he acted courageously, out of his love for the fox, for her beauty and grace and the pleasure she had given him. In the last paragraph, one reminiscent of Marjorie Kinnan Rawlings's ending in *The Yearling*, Tom writes, "I am beneath that tree again. The cold rain is beating down upon me and my heart is in my throat. And I hear, just as plainly as I heard it that August night, above the rain, beyond the years, the high clear bark of the midnight fox" (*Fox*, 159).

The plot of *The Midnight Fox* moves fairly rapidly—more quickly than the animal stories of Meindert DeJong, whose novels were still widely read when *The Midnight Fox* was published. In later novels Byars developed anecdotally related flashbacks to build character and to create humor as well as to move plots forward. Here, though, the plot has ample suspense and tension. Aunt Millie believes the fox is responsible for the loss of her turkey, and she tells Uncle Fred he has to destroy the fox. Tom knows that the beautiful black fox is responsible and will sure-ly die as a result of its depredations, but he also wants the fox to live and

desperately tries to keep Uncle Fred from finding the fox. At first Tom
thinks Uncle Fred is looking for the fox herself, but soon learns that he
knows he cannot catch the vixen but can take the baby fox to lure her
into shooting range when she comes for it.

Tom is one of Byars's first fully developed characters. While he is certainly not a namby-pamby like Sid in Mark Twain's *Tom Sawyer*, he is just
as surely not a troublemaker like Queenie in Robert Burch's *Queenie
Peavy* and not an emotionally neglected child like like Harriet in Louise
Fitzhugh's *Harriet the Spy*, two characters in children's fiction of the
1960s that raised eyebrows and caused concern among some teachers,
parents, and librarians, but not among children.

Tom has, however, some traits that put him in the ranks of fictional
characters that helped bring about the revolution in fiction for children
in the 1960s. Tom pokes fun at his parents—something children had not
done before then. He is sarcastic with his father; he tells his mother just
what he wants and does not want to do, which a child did not do in children's fiction before the 1960s.

Although Tom sounds like a smart-aleck, he is not; he is petulant and
perhaps a little spoiled, apparently used to having his way as revealed in
his refusal to go to the farm while his parents are in Europe. Even so,
Tom is bright, learning about foxes from his observations and from
answers to his questions about foxes; he is sensitive to the beauty of the
farm, its green grass, trees, the creek. Above all he is sensitive to the
beautiful and vulnerable vixen and her kit.

Even if Tom is somewhat fearful of new experiences—of swimming in
the pond, hunting with Uncle Fred, and climbing out the window to rescue the baby fox—he finds the courage and the determination to climb
down the tree and to turn the baby fox loose. His overcoming his fears
and timidity reveals his conviction and inner strength—traits that
Byars's characters will come to have in full and far greater measure as
Byars develops as a writer.

Tom foreshadows far stronger characters in Byars's fiction—characters
who will have to overcome greater obstacles than fear and timidity. One of
the virtues of Byars's fiction is that she often gives her characters the will,
courage, and determination to fight, to win, to go against the convictions
and indifferences of adults, however absurd, ingrained, and strong.

Use of humor is another aspect of *The Midnight Fox* that demonstrates
Byars's talents and growing skills as a writer. Byars's intermixing of
humor and seriousness became a hallmark of her stories for children, a
major factor in her success as a writer.

Aunt Millie and Uncle Fred are stereotypes. That they are stereotypes does not make them any less likable or any less vital and important to the story. Uncle Fred is, despite Tom's believing otherwise, a kind, gentle man, and Aunt Millie is equally kind, gentle, and compassionate. In a few strokes Byars deftly paints them through Tom's eyes so that readers see and know them as Tom perceives them.

One of the major themes of *The Midnight Fox* is that children have to be themselves; they have to be who and what they are, not who and what their parents want them to be or what parents think they ought to be. Tom's father is a coach, athletic and sure of himself; Tom is neither athletic nor sure of himself. No matter how much Tom's father wants him to be a "sport," a name he often calls Tom, Tom is not and knows and admits it candidly to himself. Byars seems to be telling young male readers that they do not have to be athletes; some people can be friends of foxes, lovers of beauty, and freers of foxes. Metaphorically and thematically, Byars perhaps is also saying that saving foxes is just as important as being a good athlete.

Another idea reflected in the story is that rare and beautiful foxes (black foxes are rare) should be defended and looked after. Byars will use defenseless animals, though not always rare ones, in other stories, giving credence to the sublimated theme that such animals often need protection.

The Midnight Fox also represents the converse of the idea that our anticipation of something is often better than the event itself. Or, to state this idea another way, sometimes the more we dislike or dread doing something that should be pleasant, our pleasure and enjoyment in the reality are intensified, frequently because of external forces. Tom does not anticipate his two months' visit to the farm; in fact, he dreads it, has secret fears about living on a farm, and sees himself in predicaments that he will be unable to cope with. Even after he arrives at the farm, he imagines himself in situations with Uncle Fred that he does not want to be in, as when he does not want to swim in the pond with Uncle Fred, fearing he will drown. Tom's fears, however, are generally unrealized. Because of the black fox, Tom's pleasure and enjoyment of the farm and his growing appreciation for Aunt Millie, Uncle Fred, and Hazeline are far greater than his fears and dreads.

The Midnight Fox is Byars's first novel with a first person point of view—one that can offer a feeling of immediacy and intimacy that third-person stories sometimes lack. A children's story in first person is somewhat risky, however, especially when the writer is nine years old. Byars,

however, makes Tom 14 when he recalls his summer on the farm, and it
is possible that a 14-year-old boy could have written the story, though its
style somewhat belies the writing of most boys of 14 and of many 10
and 20 years older.

The Summer of the Swans

Betsy Byars's seventh book, *The Summer of the Swans* (1970), is perhaps
her best-known book because it won the 1971 Newbery Medal and
because it has sustained a wide readership for more than 20 years.

During a conversation between the 14-year-old protagonist, Sara
Godfrey, and her 18-year-old sister, Wanda, Sara reveals that she is
unhappy about herself physically and emotionally and dissatisfied with
Aunt Willie and her father. Aunt Willie is somewhat crotchety and
plain-spoken or just plain tactless. Sara's father rarely comes home to
West Virginia from his job in Ohio and seems to have lost interest in his
family.

Later in the day Sara takes her 10-year-old retarded brother, Charlie,
to see the swans that have flown from a nearby lake to one near their
neighborhood. Fascinated by the swans, Charlie does not want to return
home. Late that night, restless and upset over a missing button on his
pajamas, Charlie cannot sleep; hearing a noise outside, he gets up, and at
one of the windows in his bedroom, he sees a white cat, which he thinks
is a swan. Somehow he conceives the idea that a swan has come for him.
Leaving the house and wandering off through a vacant lot, Charlie
becomes confused, unable to return home or to find the lake and the
swans. Barking dogs frighten Charlie, and he runs through trees and
tangled briars, losing one of his moccasins. Finally, near dawn, he wanders into a ravine, hopelessly lost.

Sara and Aunt Willie discover the next morning that Charlie is miss-
ing. Aunt Willie calls the police, and later in the day Sara and her friend
Mary Weicek set out to look for Charlie while a search party is being
organized. Joe Melby, the boy whom Sara has accused of stealing
Charlie's watch, his most prized possession, joins them, but not before
Mary tells Sara that Joe had not stolen Charlie's watch. Mary leaves to
give a message to the search party that Joe has found Charlie's moccasin.
Joe and Sara continue their search, and at the top of a hill overlooking
the valley and the town, Charlie answers their calls, and Sara finds him
in the ravine. After Charlie has been reunited with Aunt Willie, Joe asks
Sara to go to Bennie Hoffman's party with him.

The Summer of the Swans is a remarkable book; usually in a work of fiction, one aspect, such as theme, plot, or characterization will stand out, but in this novel, all three are outstanding. Especially remarkable and effective is Byars's characterization of Charlie and her treatment of Charlie's mental retardation.

The Summer of the Swans is among Byars's most astutely constructed novels. Once Byars presents the generating circumstances, the action of the plot moves at a rapid pace and the tension and suspense build through several threads, all related to the central theme. Although Charlie's being lost creates the most dramatic tension, Sara's unhappiness and dissatisfaction are the most important aspects in moving the story forward, if less dramatic and more subtle. Byars's characterization of Sara and her portrayal of Sara and Sara's ultimate discovery about herself and others unify the various elements and create the primary theme that unifies and solidifies the novel into a satisfyingly complete and aesthetic work of art.

In Sara Godfrey, Byars has created a complex girl, one who is so genuine and so unerringly presented that she becomes one of Byars's most fully realized female characters. Though no less appealing, Sara is more complex than Tom in *The Midnight Fox*, and both Sara and Tom are more fully developed than Dewey Martin, the protagonist in *Trouble River*, Byars's first novel presenting a somewhat fully developed realistic character.

Typical of many adolescents, Sara is unhappy about a number of things, including the color and cut of her hair and her big feet; she thinks Aunt Willie is somewhat coarse; she thinks her father should take a greater interest in his three children. Serving as a recurring motif, Sara's tennis shoes reflect her unhappiness and dissatisfaction. At first Sara likes her orange sneakers, but when Wanda points out that the orange color simply calls attention to her feet, she decides she hates them. Sara dyes the shoes, coloring them puce.

Through expository and dramatic revelation, Byars builds the character of Sara. Early in the novel Sara tells Charlie, "This has been the worst summer of my life."[2] In two passages she explains to herself why the summer is the worst: "She did not know exactly why this was true. She was doing the same things she had done last summer—walk to the Dairy Queen with her friend Mary, baby-sit for Mrs. Hodges, watch television—and yet everything was different. . . . She could never be really sure of anything this summer. One moment she was happy, and the next, for no reason, she was miserable. An hour ago she had loved her sneakers; now she detested them" (*Swans*, 13, 16).

Before her fourteenth summer, Sara "had loved her sister without envy, her aunt without finding her coarse, her brother without pity. Now all that was changed. She was filled with discontent, an anger about herself, her life, her family, that made her think she would never be content again" (*Swans*, 46).

Later that night after she and Wanda are in bed, they talk, and Wanda realizes something is bothering Sara and asks her what is wrong. Sara's answer indicates her emotional discontent. Sara says she feels "not physically awful, just plain awful. I feel like I want to start screaming and kicking and I want to jump up and tear down the curtains and rip up the sheets and hammer holes in the walls. I want to yank my clothes out of the closet and burn them and—. . . I just feel like nothing." When Wanda says that everyone at times feels like nothing, Sara's response is, "I'm not anything. I'm not cute, and I'm not pretty, and I'm not a good dancer, and I'm not smart, and I'm not popular. I'm not anything" (*Swans*, 49).

How adolescents feel about themselves, their lives, their families, about being cute, pretty, smart, and popular, is important to them. As Sara herself says, "I think how you look is the most important thing in the world. If you *look* cute, you *are* cute; if you *look* smart, you *are* smart, and if you don't look like anything, then you aren't anything" (*Swans*, 31).

Sara's dissatisfaction is also reflected in her vindictive attitude toward Joe Melby, who, she believes, stole Charlie's watch. In her anger about the watch, one day at school she puts a sign on Joe's back with "FINK" on it. While Sara and Mary search for Charlie, Sara says she has an unforgiving spirit when anyone does something mean to Charlie. "When I think somebody has done something mean to Charlie I can't forgive them. I want to keep after them and keep after them" (*Swans*, 96).

Sara's unhappiness is further indicated by her feeling left out. Mary and others have been invited to Bennie Hoffman's party, but not Sara. Sara's discontent with her life leads to the central truth of the novel. Her discontent and her discovery about herself and about life are directly related to and reinforce the theme. There are two primary sources of Sara's revelation—Charlie's being lost and found, and Sara's learning that Joe did not steal Charlie's watch and that he is kind and good.

Charlie's being lost gives Sara a far greater concern than the size of her feet or the cut of her hair; for the first time during the summer she has something to think about besides herself—she has a genuine worry and concern. With Charlie's being lost, Sara's personal unhappiness and discontent recede. Not once during the time Charlie is lost does Sara mention her looks, how she feels about her haircut, her feet, or her family; nor does she say that she is "nothing." Sara's finding Charlie in the ravine and the look on his face and his steel embrace when she descends to him in the gully tell her how much, even with his limited abilities, he loves her. When Charlie sees Sara at the top of the ravine, "a strange expression came over his face, an expression of wonder and joy and disbelief, and Sara knew that if she lived to be a hundred no one would ever look at her quite that way again." Immediately afterwards in the ravine with him, Charlie's "arms gripped her like steel" (*Swans*, 126).

Sara has felt only anger and bitterness toward Joe since Charlie lost his watch, which Sara thinks Joe stole and then returned, saying that he had found it. While Mary and Sara are in the woods looking for Charlie, Mary tells Sara that she has just learned from her mother the truth about the watch. Joe had not stolen it but had simply had gotten it from the boy who had taken it. Realizing how mean and little and unfair she has been, she says to Mary, "It makes me feel terrible. . . . Terrible!" (*Swans*, 96).

Earlier, when she has declared to Charlie that "how you look is the most important thing in the world," she recalls an essay she had written—and gotten a D on—about how looks are important. Afterwards, the teacher pointed out to her that "some of the ugliest people in the world were the smartest and kindest and cleverest" (*Swans*, 31–32).

It took Charlie's being lost and learning that Joe was not a fink to bring about Sara's enlightenment, moving her from being unhappy, miserable, and wrongheaded to accepting herself, her retarded brother, her Aunt Willie, and her father as they are, not as she might wish herself and them to be. Sara is no longer self-centered and mawkishly self-pitying. She sees that big feet, skinny legs, unbecoming haircuts, and orange sneakers are relatively unimportant in the scheme of things, but that lost and found brothers and kind boys are important.

When Sara and Joe are returning with Charlie, Sara is puzzled as to why she suddenly feels good; however, it is no puzzle for readers. Sara has found Charlie, but she has also found more. Having Charlie safe and seeing Joe as a kind, likable, and compassionate boy are far better than worrying about skinny legs, big feet, a crotchety aunt, and a disinterested father. Sara has gained insight into herself and into her real and imagined concerns. Furthermore, Joe asks Sara to go with him to Bennie Hoffman's party, giving Sara a feeling of belonging.

At the end of the novel, when Sara is talking on the telephone to her father, she has a mental vision that puts her experiences of the day and what they mean into perspective:

> A picture came into her mind, . . . and she suddenly saw life as a series of huge, uneven steps, and she saw herself on the steps, standing motionless, . . . and she had just taken an enormous step up out of the shadows, and she was standing, waiting, and there were other steps in front of her, so that she could go as high as the sky, and she saw Charlie on a flight of small difficult steps, and her father down at the bottom of some steps, just sitting and not trying to go further. She saw everyone she knew on those blinding white steps and for a moment everything was clearer than it had ever been. (*Swans*, 140)

Charlie Godfrey is a consummate fictional realization of a retarded child. Byars captures the essence of the behavior of such a child and successfully makes Charlie a logically and psychologically convincing and consistent character. Before she wrote *The Summer of the Swans* Byars felt that she was not accomplishing what she wanted to in her writing and thought about seeking another career. At the University of West Virginia Byars enrolled in classes, including special education, where she studied mentally retarded children, leading to her writing a work of fiction about a retarded child. The fruits of her study of retarded children is an uncannily accurate and unsentimental portrayal of a retarded child.[3]

In *The Sound and the Fury* William Faulkner portrays young, retarded Benjy Compson through stream of consciousness. Byars, however, uses an omniscient point of view to enter into the mind of Charlie—better for young readers than a stream-of-consciousness point of view. There are a number of instances where Byars tells readers what Charlie is thinking, and several of them deal with his watch, which, like Sara's orange sneakers, becomes a dominant motif in connection with her portrayal of Charlie: "The watch was a great pleasure to him. He had no knowledge of hours or minutes, but he liked to listen to it and to watch the small red hand moving around the dial, counting off the seconds, and it was he who remembered every morning after breakfast to have Aunt Willie wind it for him. . . . There was something about the rhythmic ticking that never failed to soothe him. The watch was a magic charm whose tiny noise and movements could block out the whole clamoring world" (*Swans*, 35, 37).

Byars's description of Charlie in the ravine shows a mentally retarded child's reactions to frustration; at the same time, the description reveals Byars's understanding and knowledge of mental retardation in children: "Suddenly something seemed to explode within Charlie, and he began to cry noisily. He threw himself on the bank and began kicking, flailing at the ground, at the invisible chipmunk [he had seen earlier], at the silent watch. He wailed, yielding in helplessness to his anguish, and his piercing screams, uttered again and again, seemed to hang in the air so that they overlapped. His fingers tore at the tree roots and dug beneath the leaves and scratched, animal-like, at the dark earth" (*Swans*, 111).

Another passage that reveals Byars's knowledge about mental retardation in children explains how they—and specifically, Charlie—need routine sameness and order in their lives. Charlie's "whole life had been built on a strict routine, and as long as this routine was kept up, he felt safe and well. The same foods, the same bed, the same furniture in the same place, the same seat on the school bus, the same class procedure were all important to him. But always there could be the unexpected, the dreadful surprise that would topple his carefully constructed life in an instant" (*Swans*, 122).

There are a few similarities between *The Summer of the Swans* and Hans Christian Andersen's *The Ugly Duckling*. Although Sara's family and friends never overtly ostracize her or treat her cruelly, she does feel a sense of ostracism, similar to the feelings of the cygnet. In the beginnings of both stories, the "ugly duckling" is unhappy and miserable; both girl and cygnet suffer a sense of being different and isolated. In the end, both are happy, and both have a sense of self worth they lacked at the beginning.

Unlike the Ugly Duckling, however, who has been transformed physically and emotionally at the end of the story, Sara has been transformed only emotionally; she still has the same skinny legs, the same crooked nose, and the same unbecoming haircut. Perhaps readers should not make too much of these similarities. Whether Byars was conscious of the similarities between her story and Andersen's is a moot point, but her using swans in her story may remind readers of Andersen's story. The swans have no particular symbolic meaning in the story, but how they came to be in the story is interesting. As an undergraduate, Byars spent two years at Furman University, which has a small lake with swans on its Greenville, South Carolina, campus. While working on the novel Byars received an alumni bulletin from Furman picturing the swans on the lake. She moved the swans and the lake to West Virginia for her story.

One of the most unusual aspects of *The Summer of the Swans* is that the action covers about 24 hours. A writer runs a serious risk in presenting an action in such a short period of time. In less skillful, less talented hands, the rather drastic change that takes place in Sara's mental outlook during 24 hours would be incredible and artificial, the kind of resolution to conflict known as deus ex machina. But Byars uses Charlie's being lost to make Sara's change credible and realistic; it would take a drastic and near-tragic loss to bring about a different outlook in a person in a 24-hour period.

The House of Wings

In *The House of Wings* (1972) 10-year-old Sammy and his parents, Lucille and Harry, leave Alabama for Detroit, where Harry hopes to find work. On the way they stop one night in Ohio at Lucille's father's home. The next morning when Sammy wakes late, he learns his parents have gone, planning for him to go to Detroit later.

Hurt and enraged because his parents have left him, Sammy blames his grandfather, refusing to believe him when he tells Sammy his parents have left without him. In his rage, Sammy immediately leaves for Detroit with his grandfather chasing him and calling him "Boy." When Sammy comes to the superhighway, he hides in a culvert, but his grandfather finds him. Sammy runs through another culvert under the second lane, and still his grandfather comes for him.

Hungry, hot, and weak because he's had nothing to eat but a Moon Pie and an RC Cola since the afternoon before, Sammy hides behind a deserted shack. Suddenly, his grandfather seems to have disappeared; Sammy thinks he's hiding, planning to sneak up and grab him. Directly, his grandfather calls him from the woods, and even though Sammy is afraid his grandfather is using a trick to catch him, he senses an urgency in his grandfather's call. In the woods he finds his grandfather near some undergrowth watching a wounded sandhill crane.

Thinking the bird cannot fly because of a bad wing, Sammy's grandfather decides to try to catch the bird, but not before he and Sammy exchange angry words. When Sammy tells his grandfather he does not care if the bird dies, his grandfather tells Sammy about the time he killed a redbird with a rock and how much it hurt him to have killed the bird. The story makes no immediate impression on Sammy, who declares, "I hope he *does* die."[4] Sammy throws a rock at the crane and misses, but his act sets his grandfather off: " 'Well, you just go on to Detroit, hear? Just head on out of here. Keep on running as long as you want to. Ain't nobody going to try and stop you this time.' He made a sharp shooing gesture with both hands. 'Go on. You don't belong here' " (*Wings*, 48–49).

After telling Sammy to leave a few times, his grandfather's anger leaves him quickly, and Sammy's "anger began to go out of him, not as quickly as it had his grandfather, but slowly, jerkily, bit by bit" (*Wings*, 52). Sammy's grandfather catches the bird and carries it to his house, and after he and Sammy give the crane food and water, the old man discovers that the crane is blind.

Despite his claim he is not interested in the crane, Sammy is interested, not only in the crane, but also in his grandfather's owl, geese, and parrot (whose only words are "Good-bye" and "Where's Papa?"), as well as other birds his grandfather has had. Although Sammy does not want his grandfather to know it, Sammy's interest in and concern for the crane grow, and the next morning, he joins his grandfather in carrying the crane to the creek. In the slow-moving water, the crane takes its first steps since its capture. Sammy catches a frog and finally entices the crane into eating it. Moving to the opposite side of the creek, the crane begins to dig in the mud, finding and eating insects and roots. Sammy finally addresses his grandfather as "Papa" and asks Papa to call him Sammy.

The House of Wings is Byars's fourth realistic story in which animals play important parts, albeit in different degrees. Byars's portrayal of animals is accurate, and although she carefully researches the animal she is writing about at the time, it is nonetheless obvious that she has an affinity for animals, especially dogs, as well as being a keen observer of them. While the animals in *The House of Wings*, in this case, birds, do not take center stage, they do play a vital role in the story as Sammy's grandfather is unabashedly and unapologetically a lover of birds.

The plot is tightly knit and moves rapidly because it centers on Sammy and the crane and their relationship with Sammy's grandfather. Compared with other protagonists in the major novels of Byars, Sammy is a relatively flat but dynamic character. He is obnoxiously rude to and indifferent toward his grandfather. His rudeness can be attributed not only to his anger at being left behind but also to his upbringing, which has been sorry at best: "It seemed to Sammy that his life had been, up until this morning [when he discovers his parents have left him], one long flowing time. For ten years he had been free. He had been part of the world the way a bird is or an animal. He had gone where he wanted and had done the things that pleased him. He had come home when he was ready to eat, and slept, if he liked, curled up on the sofa like a puppy. His parents had allowed him to raise himself because he was the last of eight children and they were worn out" (*Wings*, 12–13).

Another indication that Sammy has never had much direction or discipline comes in a flashback when he recalls getting a report card on which his teacher had written, "Sammy needs to work on his personal hygiene." When his mother explained what the statement meant, she looked at "him closely for the first time in weeks," and readers learn he has not even washed his hands for a week, though his mother does not realize it. She makes him take a bath and for a few days keeps after him about bathing; "then after a week, his mother stopped noticing and he had stopped washing" (*Wings*, 116–18).

In the course of his few hours with his grandfather, however, Sammy is given a sense of direction and some discipline. Although an indifferent and unorthodox kind of discipline, it is about the only discipline Sammy has ever had.

Sammy "was not a polite boy" (*Wings*, 17), and his rudeness and impoliteness show when his grandfather tells him his parents have left him. In his anger and frustration as he runs away, Sammy calls his grandfather a liar several times, implying that his grandfather has done something to his parents (*Wings*, 25–26). Sammy's rudeness, anger, and sorry upbringing cause him to be distrustful and cynical toward his grandfather. When his grandfather tells him the the bird he has found is a crane, Sammy does not believe him: "Sammy had never seen such a bird. He had never heard of one either, and he did not trust his grandfather's knowledge. 'A what?' he asked. A faintly scornful smile pulled down the corners of his mouth" (*Wings*, 40).

Despite his scorn, rudeness, and cynicism, Sammy begins to soften under the spell of his grandfather and his birds as well as his grandfather's stories about other birds he has had. Sammy's attitude begins to change. Soon after Sammy's and his grandfather's bitter exchange when his grandfather tells him to go on to Detroit, and during the last few minutes before his grandfather captures the crane, Sammy begins to feel different, to feel a kinship with his grandfather, and becomes less impudent and scornful: "Suddenly he was confused. It was not just the strangeness of the land. It was everything. It seemed to him a hundred years ago when he had been on the way to Detroit with his parents" (*Wings*, 70).

Sammy's grandfather, whom readers know only as "Sammy's grandfather" and as "Papa" because that's what his parrot calls him, is one of Byars's admirable portrayals of older men and women. Byars imbues the old man with strong feeling about the preciousness of life, which he learned as a boy when he killed a redbird. After he picked up the bird, he tells Sammy he "never felt any heavier weight than that dead bird" (*Wings*, 46). When Sammy learns that the crane is blind and wonders if his grandfather will kill the crane, his grandfather says, "Life turns out to be a lot more precious than you think. There ain't nothing more precious. . . . I know it right now just by being an old man, or I wouldn't have carried that crane all the way home, and I'm not killing this crane if there's anything else I can do" (*Wings*, 95–96).

The old man's birds, past and present, are his consuming passion; he tells Sammy that he has "had birds living with me the best part of my life, but I never went out and caught one" (*Wings*, 54). The old man's birds are more important to him than people, more important than his own children; his passion for birds is an obsession, made clear when he declares to Sammy, " 'Everyone of them birds that stayed with me is more real to me than the people I've known. . . . I can't even get some of my children straight in my mind. . . . I never have been able to tell the girls one from the other, and I got a son living in Louisiana that I wouldn't know if he jumped out from behind that bush yonder.' He shook his head, 'But, boy, I'll tell you something. I could pick my owl and my blackbird and my gray parrot and my canary and my wild ducks out of a thousand' " (*Wings*, 74).

From the dead redbird to the wounded crane, birds represent the preciousness of life to the old man, indicated by the care he has given them all. His love and care toward the birds parallel his care and concern for Sammy, his accepting Sammy as he is—spoiled, impudent, cynical, and hurt. Both Sammy and the crane are wounded; the bird is blind and hurt, and Sammy is figuratively blind and emotionally hurt; both need rehabilitation. Both are scared, hungry, and need help. Sammy and the crane need the kind of sustenance that the old man supplies—food and water for the crane, and patience, admonition, and example for Sammy. Once in the creek the blind crane manages to find food for itself and will likely survive.

Sammy's grandfather's interest in Sammy is not overwhelming, nor is it sentimental. He deals with his hurt grandson the same way he deals with wounded birds: naturally. The old man does not set out to reform

Sammy, but Sammy begins to change; he hesitantly begins to respect and admire his grandfather. The old man's birds, the crane, and his stories about his birds work wonders in Sammy, and by the end of the story he seeks the approval and commendation of his grandfather, who wittingly or unwittingly, gives it. When Sammy asks him to watch him swim, Sammy makes "a blaze of water" as he tries to swim. When he asks his grandfather how he did, he replies, "That was fine, Sammy." His grandfather's praise for his attempt causes Sammy to confess the truth, something he would not have done when he first came to his grandfather: " 'I can't do it very well now, but I'll get better. Right now I'm going to find another frog.' He moved back to the bank. He felt good and clean at last. He smoothed his red hair down on his head. 'I'll get better. Don't you worry about that' " (*Wings*, 142).

One of the key ideas in this passage is that Sammy feels "good and clean at last." His swim is a kind of baptism. He is ostensibly referring to physical cleanliness, but perceptive readers realize Sammy unconsciously refers to his spiritual and emotional cleanliness, too. Another key idea is that he will "get better." When he tells the truth about his swimming and claims he will get better at swimming, readers also understand that Sammy will get better emotionally under the care of his old, wild grandfather, who recognizes the preciousness of life even in spoiled brats.

All through the story the grandfather has never called Sammy anything but "Boy," and Sammy has not called his grandfather anything. At the end of the story Sammy wants "his grandfather to know him the way he knew his birds . . . to pick him out of a thousand boys the way he could pick out the blackbird, the owl, the wild ducks" (*Wings*, 140–41). Sammy calls the old man "Papa," and at Sammy's request his grandfather calls his grandson Sammy. It is as if before then neither had seen the other as a person to be called by a name. Calling each other by name, however, endows them both with a dignity and humanity that neither had recognized before.

It may appear unrealistic that Sammy changes as much as he does in a little over 24 hours. Given Sammy's background and the circumstances that bring about the change, however, his change is logical and realistic. He has had little direction or discipline during his 10 years. He is worn out after riding two days in the back of his father's pickup, and he is hungry. He is shocked by the appearance of his grandfather and his grandfather's strange and frightening house and way of life. Sammy's rudeness and impoliteness result in part from his immediate shock and hurt and his life-long habit of having his way, doing what he wants to do when he wants. After the initial shock and hurt, however, Sammy begins to see his grandfather and his surroundings in a different light. His grandfather's easy and natural discipline, his attitude toward Sammy and the birds, his philosophy about the "preciousness of life," and their finding and caring for the wounded and blind crane create an atmosphere for change and growth—psychologically motivated and realistic.

The 18th Emergency

Better known as Mouse, 12-year-old Benjie Fawley of *The 18th Emergency* (1973) has a habit of labeling things. In the hallway where he sleeps on a day bed, he has written near a cobweb hanging from the light fixture, "UNSAFE FOR PUBLIC SWINGING and [has] drawn an arrow to the cobweb."[5] On Thursday at school, as he walks down the hall, he comes to a wall chart showing the evolution of people. On an impulse, he writes the name of Marv Hammerman, the school bully, and then draws an arrow from Hammerman's name to the picture of Neanderthal man. Turning around, he sees Marv Hammerman reading what he's written. Mouse "could remember turning and looking into Hammerman's eyes. It was such a strange, troubling moment that Mouse was unable to think about it" (*18th*, 23).

Knowing that Hammerman will wait for him after school, Mouse runs all the way home. He tells his mother that some boys are going to kill him, but gets little sympathy from her. To get his mind off his fear and dread, he begins to think of emergencies for escaping from dangerous animals—a lion, an enraged bull, a boa constrictor, and others, but none of the emergencies give him relief from his worry. After his supper of only four lima beans, he goes outside the apartment house to visit with his best friend, Ezzie Weimer; he tells Ezzie the whole story. Ezzie offers sympathy, and in his eyes, Mouse "had taken on a fine tragic dimension" (*18th*, 29).

A little later, while Mouse is bringing Mr. Casino, a stroke victim and neighbor, home from his daughter's, Ezzie comes running down the street to tell Mouse that Hammerman and his friend in the black sweatshirt, Peachie, are in the neighborhood. Mouse tries to get Ezzie to take Mr. Casino home, but Ezzie refuses. Mouse takes Mr. Casino into the entrance of the next apartment building to avoid Hammerman and Peachie. Mr. Casino becomes restless and makes for the door several times, but Mouse manages to stop him until Mr. Casino ignores Mouse and leaves. Mouse follows, and to his relief neither Hammerman nor

Peachie is on the street. Mouse goes back to relieving his mind by thinking up emergencies, and after he goes to bed, he falls asleep trying to
think of Emergency Fifteen.

On Friday morning he tells his mother he's sick, but he does not have
a temperature; she sends him to school. He gets to school late, spends a
miserable morning trying to avoid Hammerman, and succeeds until
Hammerman finally catches him after lunch and says, "I'll see you after
school" (*18th*, 71). In math class Mrs. Romanoski tells Mouse he looks
sick and sends him to the office. Mouse is sent home and again avoids a
confrontation with Hammerman though the fear and dread remain as
strong as ever. On Saturday morning Mouse goes out looking for
Hammerman. In front of the old Rialto Theater, Mouse meets
Hammerman and Peachie. Hammerman hits him five times, twice in the
stomach, once on his breast bone, and twice on the nose, which bleeds
profusely. When Hammerman asks him if he's had enough, Mouse
replies, "If you have" (*18th*, 112). He says thanks and leaves, feeling better than he's felt since Thursday.

The 18th Emergency is a hilarious story with a serious point, the first
Byars novel to combine almost flawlessly humor and seriousness—a
combination she will develop consummately in some of her later novels.
Furthermore, *The 18th Emergency* deals with an almost universal concern
of children: dealing with a bully.

The humor in the novel is from many sources, but mainly from the
predicament that Mouse Fawley finds himself in and from his best
friend, Ezzie Weimer, and secondarily from Mouse's penchant or habit of
labeling various things, from his and Ezzie's emergency escapes from
imaginary encounters with wild animals and from funny situational and
anecdotal flashbacks and incidents.

Opening with Mouse's race for home from school to escape
Hammerman, Byars literally grabs a reader's attention and curiosity,
immediately arousing suspense with her picture of a boy racing home in
fear and announcing to his mother, "Some boys are going to kill me"
(*18th*, 9). This exaggerated claim Mouse's mother immediately doubts,
as any normal mother might, and she asks what he has done to the boys
to make them chase him. Getting no sympathy from his mother, he
seeks relief in various ways, including recalling the solutions to or
escapes from the imaginary encounters with wild animals. But whatever
Mouse does or whatever he thinks about offers no relief from his worry
over having set the school bully against him. There is no relief for
Mouse—not from Ezzie, not from television, not from his father who

calls home from his job as a truck driver, not from Mr. or Mrs. Casino, not from anybody or anything.

The labels that Mouse writes everywhere are funny and help to delineate his character. At a hole in his tennis shoe, he writes "AIR VENT" with an arrow pointing to the hole (*18th*, 10). Near a crack in the hallway between his parents and the Casinos' apartments, he "had written TO OPEN BUILDING TEAR ALONG THIS LINE and [had] drawn an arrow to the crack" (*18th*, 33). At a hole in the plaster by the doorway of the entrance to his apartment building, "Mouse had once drawn an arrow to the hole and had written DROP COINS HERE BEFORE EXITING" (*18th*, 57).

Byars's authorial comment that Ezzie "was the only good friend Mouse had ever had" (*18th*, 52) shows him as somewhat introverted, but his labels reflect a degree of extroversion; they also show that he has a wry sense of humor. Byars's use of this kind of device to help delineate character is reminiscent of Dickens's and other writers' use of tags to develop character as Dickens does with Miss Murdstone in *Great Expectations*; Miss Murdstone is a cold and cruel woman whom Dickens surrounds with metal objects to emphasize the metallic hardness of her nature. Mouse's labeling shows not only his wry sense of humor, but it also shows Byars's knowledge of children and the things they typically do and her talent and skill for incorporating such traits into her stories.

The emergencies are not only funny but they also reveal Byars's knowledge of how children sometimes think illogically. When she was writing *The 18th Emergency*, she asked her own children to help her think of animals for the imaginary encounters. They came up with several that she used, but some of them were too bizarre. Although her children helped with the animals, the improbabilities of the solutions that Ezzie and Mouse use in subjugating the animals are largely Byars's own (Int). It is the boys' remarkable but totally impractical solutions that show Byars knows how children think. The solution for the third emergency, an "Unexpected Charge of an Enraged Bull," is to get in the blind spot in the center of the bull's vision, "so when being charged by a bull, you try to line yourself up with this blind spot." "Fat people can't do it, Mouse," Ezzie explains. "That's why you never see any fat bullfighters. You and I can. We just turn sideways like this, see, get in the blind spot and wait" (*18th*, 13). What Ezzie does not think of, and which shows that Byars knows how children sometimes think, is that the bull is likely going to keep charging in the same direction. Other solutions to the dangerous animal attacks have similar childlike lapses of logic.

In his fine essay "Little Bit of Ivory—Betsy Byars," David Rees finds flaws of improbability in *The 18th Emergency*, including the "emergencies" that Mouse and Ezzie dream up: "the language and concepts of the seventeen emergencies are too unreal, too amusing."[6] He is indeed correct in saying they are unreal; Byars never intended them to be any thing else. She knows they are unreal, but that is the point; they are unreal because Mouse is grasping at straws for relief from his worrying about a bully's revenge and to keep from facing a truth that he cannot even think about or face until near the end of the story. When child or adult is sick with worry and cannot think about anything but the worry, the imagination can and often does offer temporary respite in wild and improbable visions and solutions. The preposterous and hilarious emergencies of Mouse and Ezzie also offer respite to child readers, many of whom, if not most, have confronted bullies, who come in all sizes, ages, and guises, and who are rarely overgrown, older hulks. Realistically, Hammerman is a bully of flesh and blood; symbolically, he is all the bullies lurking in our psyches. Although Rees writes for children and is a thoughtful critic, perhaps he has never had a bully or has forgotten what it is like to face a bully, but Byars apparently has and knows from her own experiences or from those of her children. *The 18th Emergency* remains one of Byars's most widely read novels, and perhaps one reason is that nearly everyone has a bully, imagined or real, human or otherwise. A little humor and nonsense can and do help bring real and symbolic bullies down to size.

While Mouse's labels and his and Ezzie's fanciful emergency solutions are funny and offer comic relief during Mouse's—and the reader's—agonizing Thursday night, Friday, and Saturday morning, Byars frequently relieves the agony of Mouse's ordeal with delightful and funny situations and anecdotes. On Thursday night while Mouse and Ezzie are discussing how Mouse came to antagonize the older and larger Hammerman and the awful blows Mouse will likely receive, the reader learns that while Mouse has been hit in the stomach four times in the past, Ezzie has never been hit because he's an expert dodger: "Sometimes his mother chased him through the apartment striking at him while he dodged and ducked, crying, 'Look out, Mom, look out now! You're going to hit me!'" (*18th*, 24). Another funny incident occurs on Friday morning when Mouse claims he's too sick to go to school. Mouse's mother puts a thermometer in his mouth. Mouse knows he has no fever, but he tries to influence the thermometer to his advantage by "rubbing it with his tongue just in case the friction might somehow cause the mercury to rise" (*18th*, 59).

Irrepressible Ezzie offers lots of fun and respite from bullies, Mouse's or a reader's own. Byars captures the essence of some children's enthusiasm and specifically Ezzie's grand irrepressibility when the class is discussing King Arthur, knighthood, and honor. At the back of the room, "swinging his hand in the air like an upside-down pendulum," Ezzie finally despairs and yells, "Mr. Stein! Mr. Stein!" Mr. Stein ignores Ezzie, but "Ezzie could wait no longer to join in the discussion. Still waving his hand in the air he made a generous offer. 'Ask me anything you want to about honor, Mr. Stein, and I'll tell you' " (*18th*, 66).

Although Ezzie is sympathetic about Mouse's plight, he's not above having a little fun at Mouse's expense by giving Mouse a sly dig about his concern over Hammerman. Ezzie wants Mouse to play basketball, but Mouse is afraid Hammerman might show up. Ezzie says, " 'You can't ruin your whole life just because of Hammerman. Besides, if he shows up, you can just go in the grocery store and pretend to be buying something.' He paused, then added with a little smile, 'Band-Aids' " (*18th*, 81). This is just one of hundreds of places throughout the Byars canon that shows Byars's understanding of children and human nature. Only a good friend could make such a crack.

In another incident revealing Byars's knowledge of children, the math teacher, Mrs. Romanoski, asks Ezzie to put the first problem of the homework on the board. In the ensuing discussion between him and Mrs. Romanoski, Ezzie reveals himself typical of many students who do not always do their homework. It is a scene all students can enjoy not only because it is a common predicament but also because even when uncomfortable and embarrassed, Ezzie remains himself. He squirms under Mrs. Romanoski's close scrutiny because he, never at a loss for an instant excuse, confesses right away, "I didn't have time to study much last night because my sister was sick. She made me put out the light." Without comment, Mrs. Romanoski replies, " 'Put the first problem on the board, please.' Ezzie picked up the chalk and looked carefully at his book. . . . [He] put the chalk to his lips. He appeared to be ready to drink a vial of white liquid, perhaps the 'smart' medicine he was always hoping some scientists would discover—one sip and instant smartness. He said regretfully, 'This was the one problem I didn't get, Mrs. Romanoski, I remember now. I got all the others, but this one stumped me.' " Mrs. Romanoski points out that it is the same as Problem 2.

Blankly surprised, Ezzie finally begins putting the problem on the board, making it a problem in addition. Mrs. Romanoski points out his mistake, and he asks if she's kidding him. He then wants to know if they are looking at the same problem—and then "in an enlightened voice," he asks, "What *page?*" Taking another "sip of chalk," he says, "Wait a minute, let me read this thing again" (*18th*, 72–74). Because Mouse looks sick, Mrs. Romanoski turns her attention to him, temporarily letting Ezzie off his hot seat.

One of the funniest episodes in the book occurs in a flashback that comes up when Ezzie and Mouse are talking about the times Mouse had been hit. The boys in Mouse and Ezzie's class decide to put all the girls into garbage cans. Unknown to Mouse, who has cornered Viola Angotti, the principal has caught all the other boys; and although the playground has become quiet, it does not register with Mouse, who calls for help, not once but twice. Viola Angotti is not one to be violated with impunity: "Nobody's putting *me* in no garbage can." Mouse calls for help a third time. Viola takes a step forward and "socked him in the stomach so hard that he had doubled over and lost his lunch. As she walked past his crumpled body she had said again, 'Nobody's putting me in no garbage can.' It had sounded like one of the world's basic truths. The sun will rise. The tides will flow. Nobody's putting Viola Angotti in no garbage can" (*18th*, 26–27).

Although Byars puts considerable humor into Mouse's ordeal, she also handles it realistically. His fear of Marv Hammerman is perfectly natural because Hammerman is older and larger than the other children in the sixth grade. Ezzie reminds Mouse, "He's flunked a lot" (*18th*, 22). And Hammerman has a mean reputation; after all, "there was only one Hammerman in the world, just as there had been only one Hitler" (*18th*, 19).

Making the ordeal harder for Mouse is his sensitivity, revealed in his attitude toward Ezzie's sympathy (which nearly causes Mouse to cry). In the game of checkers with Mr. Casino, who plays slowly and tediously because of the stroke he has had, Byars shows Mouse's awareness of other people's needs when he asks Mr. Casino if he wants to play a second game and then offers to let Mr. Casino set up the board: "he pushed all the checkers across to Mr. Casino and said gently, 'You set them up this time, will you?'" (*18th*, 99). It is, finally, partly Mouse's sensitivity that makes him act honorably toward Hammerman.

But perhaps the best evidence of Mouse's sensitivity is his at first unconscious realization that he has done something to Marv Hammerman that he should not have. When he first relates the episode of the wall chart to Ezzie, Mouse recalls the look in Hammerman's eyes, something he does not yet understand and cannot verbalize or even think about: "He could remember turning and looking into Hammerman's eyes. It was such a strange, troubling moment that Mouse was unable to think about it" (*18th*, 23).

On Friday night while he's playing checkers with Mr. Casino, he recalls again the moment when he saw Hammerman's eyes. Forcing himself to think about it, he realizes that he has a kinship, an understanding about Hammerman, that he does not want to face. Hammerman's eyes tell Mouse in an instant of shocked recognition that they both have the capacity for being hurt. Slumping and sinking into his chair while Mr. Casino makes his tediously slow move, Mouse "knew now what troubled him [about the look in Hammerman's eyes]. He had felt somehow close to Hammerman in that first terrible moment. He had known how Hammerman felt. It had been the same way he had felt when everyone first started calling him Mouse. They had been united for a moment, Mouse and Neanderthal man" (*18th*, 96–97). With the dejected feeling that comes with recognizing wrong, Mouse knows he has behaved dishonorably toward Hammerman.

The serious point Byars makes in the novel is that honor often calls for people to accept the responsibility for and to suffer the consequences of their mistakes. Specifically, Mouse has to suffer the consequences of his mistake of demeaning the school bully. While the novel's humor, suspense, and serious point make an almost flawless narrative, Mouse's realization that Hammerman is as vulnerable as he is and Byars's treatment of Mouse's honorable encounter—the eighteenth emergency—with Hammerman and his buddy, Peachie, make the novel a superior one in her canon.

So that he can restore Hammerman's honor, Mouse goes out on Saturday morning to look for Hammerman to receive the blows he feels he somehow deserves. After all, Mouse has already decided that "survival called for keeping perfectly quiet. If it was natural to run, the best thing to do was to stand still. Whatever was the hardest, that was what you had to do sometimes to survive. The hardest thing of all, . . . was not running" (*18th*, 88). And Mouse does not run; he goes out to look for Hammerman on the streets.

Superior in cleverness, intellect, and sensitivity, Mouse has behaved underhandedly, has taken advantage of Hammerman's vulnerability and his inability to fight intellectually, just as Hammerman had taken physical advantage of others with his superior size and strength. During the rather one-sided fight, Mouse restores Hammerman's honor, and Byars reinforces the idea of Hammerman's vulnerability. Hammerman offers none of the typical macho remarks of a bully; in fact, Hammerman does not say anything until after he has delivered five blows to Mouse; and then he asks Mouse if he's had enough, and Mouse answers, "If you have." Hammerman's friend, Peachie, like a true macho bully, misunderstands Mouse's answer and points out, " 'Man, he can keep going like this all morning. . . .' Hammerman lifted one hand and opened it a little as if he were releasing something. It was a strange gesture"—a gesture of release signifying Hammerman knows his honor has been restored. Mouse thinks, "He saw it now as an old-fashioned matter of honor. He, Mouse, had dishonored Marv Hammerman, and now Hammerman had to say when his honor was restored" (*18th*, 111–12).

In Peachie and Hammerman's friendship, Byars may be indirectly making a statement about bullies in general. Peachie may be just as vulnerable as Mouse and Hammerman. He is too small to fight on his own, depending on his larger, stronger friend to deliver the blows while he stands on the sidelines offering the swaggering comments of a bully. As wrong as their despicable behavior is and as much as we may deplore it, bullies are bullies because they need to uphold their honor even though their means are dishonorable.

David Rees also questions the plausibility of Mouse's honorable behavior: Mouse's "acceptance of being beaten up as a matter of honor does not ring true. He does not, in fact, owe a debt of honor—Marv, a junior version of the Incredible Hulk, may well be annoyed that Mouse has written 'Marv Hammerman' under a picture of Neanderthal Man, but hitting Mouse until the blood flows is not, by any standards except those of revenge justice, a way of retaliation the reader should be asked to approve" (Rees, 35). Asking readers to approve of Hammerman's "hitting Mouse until the blood flows" is not the point and not what Byars is asking for; she does not ask readers to approve of Hammerman's cruelty. She is asking readers to see that Mouse behaves honorably and that, in the final analysis, even in his retaliation of "revenge justice," Marv Hammerman has a sense of honor, however slight.

Furthermore, for Mouse and Hammerman, as a stereotype and a symbol, to do any less would make them characters altogether different from what they are and as Byars has built their characters and as readers know them. For Mouse and Hammerman to behave in any other way than they do would ring false. Mouse's accepting the blows is realistic because Byars has demonstrated that Mouse is sensitively aware of the wrong he has done to Hammerman and that Mouse is honorable.

While Byars makes her serious point strong and clear in the novel and in the fight between Mouse and Hammerman, her narration of the moments before and during the fight is a masterful orchestration of tension and suspense leading to the crescendo of the fight with booming timpani, trumpeting horns, and crashing cymbals, reinforcing and strengthening her serious point. She builds the tension and suspense in various ways. By having Mouse look at his watch every few minutes she shows how tense he is. By showing his nervous movements described with short, staccato phrases, Byars reveals Mouse's increasing tenseness: "He pulled down his jacket, smoothed his hair, hitched up his pants, kept his hands busy. . . . He pulled at his ear lobe, wiped his nose, zipped his jacket higher" (*18th*, 105). She uses the bright sunlight to heighten the tension, having Mouse note that it is a bright Saturday morning as soon as he wakes. Stopping at Stumpy's, a pizza and pinball place, Mouse looks through the window: "He couldn't see anything at first because his eyes were still accustomed to the bright light outside" (*18th*, 103–4). A little later the sunlight becomes "blinding" (*18th*, 105). When the three boys meet in front of the Rialto theater "the sun went behind a cloud, and it was suddenly dim" (*18th*, 107).

The fight does not last long. Mouse, with his nose bleeding, leaves the the theater and walks down Fourth Street, feeling as if "he was . . . walking across some dusty foreign field . . . [seeing] gold and scarlet tournament flags snapping in the wind. There would be plumes and trumpets and horses in bright trappings. Honor would be a simple thing again and so vital that people would talk of it wherever they went. He felt as if a vanished age had risen up like a huge wave and washed over him. . . . He looked at his watch. It was 10:13" (*18th*, 113–14).

Byars wrote this scene while flying through a bad storm that caused the plane to rock and bump. Her own tenseness comes through in her writing and enhances the tension leading up to and including the fight. Like Mouse, she kept looking at her watch every few minutes and tried to keep her hands busy with her pen in those tense moments (Int).

Robert Grossman's illustrations for the book are superficial and do not do the story justice. Grossman's illustrations reflect only the humorous aspects of the story with exaggerated and out-of-proportion bodies; they reveal nothing about the serious undertone of the story. The illustrations show that sometimes artists and editors can misinterpret a story by emphasizing only one aspect and by choosing an inappropriate style of art.

After the Goat Man

In this 1974 story Ira Gryshevich, the Goat Man, has been driven off his land to make way for a highway cloverleaf. His life is and has been the wooded piece of land on which his cabin sits—a cabin hewn from the trees of his land.

Forced off his land and into a concrete-block unit in a housing project, Mr. Gryshevich sits for three days in the blind-darkened new house; he does not eat and does not speak to his grandson Figgy. With angry shouts, he drives any child off who comes into his yard. One afternoon, on the day the story takes place, while Figgy plays Monopoly with Ada Harrison and Harold V. Coleman, his grandfather takes his shotgun and goes back to his cabin, not yet demolished, though all the trees around it have been bulldozed. Returning home, Figgy finds his grandfather has gone and has no idea where he is. He walks back to tell Ada and Harold that he cannot play Monopoly; when he reluctantly tells them why, they realize that Figgy's grandfather and "the Goat Man" are the same person, because they have just heard on the radio that the Goat Man has gone back to his cabin, threatening to shoot anyone who tries to get him out.

Ada decides that she and Harold will help Figgy with his grandfather, famous in the town because of his refusal to give up his land and because Pepper and Brownie, two pet goats, had followed him about like dogs and had caused people to refer to him as the Goat Man. Deciding to go on their bicycles, Ada offers to lend Figgy one of hers. Afraid of bicycles, Figgy leaves immediately, although for several minutes Ada and Harold do not realize Figgy has left. After a time they catch up with him, already on to the new, unopened highway; they persuade him to ride with Harold. Going fast down a hill, Harold loses control. Far ahead at the top of the next hill, Ada looks back and sees Figgy lying on the pavement; leaving her bicycle and running back to help, she finds Harold half-conscious and helps him up and discovers Figgy has broken his leg. After Ada rouses Figgy and makes him as comfortable as she can, Harold volunteers to go for Mr. Gryshevich and trudges off toward the cabin while Ada stays with Figgy. When Mr. Gryshevich and Harold get to Figgy and Ada, Harold goes to a little grocery and calls an ambulance and Ada's father. At the hospital, Dr. Harrison sets Figgy's leg, but

Figgy refuses to stay overnight in the hospital and goes home with his grandfather.

With its skillful structure, its theme and subject, its delineation of a variety of characters, its combination of humor and poignancy, and its powerful emotion, *After the Goat Man* is among Byars's finest novels.

A sketchy summary does no more than refresh the memory of a reader who has read a story, and it cannot begin to do justice to such a carefully and expertly crafted story as *After the Goat Man*. Byars weaves her story and develops her characters around the subject of change and subsequent upheaval and their effects. Byars seems to be suggesting that change and upheaval can be both painful and beneficial. It can bring pain, grief, and depression to some, while to others it can bring new insights, maturity, and greater empathy and understanding.

Change and upheaval bring considerable pain to Ira Gryshevich, the Goat Man, and they change him in the process. For two years he has fought the superhighway builders, but in the end they bulldoze all the trees around his cabin and then move him and Figgy to a concrete-block housing project. For someone like Ira Gryshevich, who has lived all his life on his own land in a cabin he's apparently built himself, such an upheaval can only be painful. From the beginning, the impending change and upheaval are difficult for him. Figgy thinks of his grandfather as being like wild animals that fight to protect their territories. The first time a representative comes to tell Mr. Gryshevich and Figgy that "right where the cabin was sitting, . . . was going to be a giant cloverleaf turnoff," Mr. Gryshevich orders the man out, declaring the land his. He "swelled up like a frog . . . his . . . voice came out as deep as if it were coming from a cave. 'Get out. Get *out!*' " The man starts to explain, but Mr. Gryshevich interrupts: " 'Get off! Get out of here! This is my land!' It was like thunder rumbling down the sides of the mountain. 'This is *my land!*' "[7]

After Mr. Gryshevich and Figgy move into the housing project, Byars makes the old man's pain evident through his behavior. For three days he shuts the doors and windows, draws the blinds, and does not eat. When children come into the yard, he runs them off, shouting, "Get off! Get out of here!" (*Goat*, 22). He sits slumped on the sofa in the dark front room and neither speaks to Figgy nor acknowledges his presence. Change and upheaval are hard and painful for Mr. Gryshevich, and in his anger and bitterness and pain he takes his shotgun and goes back to the cabin and locks himself in. With understated simplicity, Figgy tells Ada and Harold, "The cabin and the land are very important to him" (*Goat*, 49).

Although Figgy reacts joyfully to the news the highway representative brings and although he likes living in the new house with running water and other conveniences, the change in his grandfather worries and frightens him: "The trouble with his grandfather had been a source of pain to Figgy during the past year. His grandfather had been, up until the trouble over the highway, a stern but gentle man, a sort of hermit" (*Goat*, 38). He cannot understand the change in his grandfather or why his grandfather does not like the new house. Figgy "would have liked living in this house, he would have liked the whole neighborhood if it weren't for his grandfather. It was the nicest house Figgy had ever lived in. He couldn't see why his grandfather hated it" (*Goat*, 27). Figgy tries to coax his grandfather out of his depression and misery, "trying to interest him in the new appliances. . . . He had suggested that his grandfather sit out on the porch and watch the traffic go by" (*Goat*, 26).

After Figgy learns from Harold and Ada his grandfather has gone back to the cabin with a shotgun, he leaves immediately to go to the cabin himself. Although Harold and Ada say they will go with him on their bicycles with Figgy riding on one of Ada's, Figgy leaves without them because he's afraid of riding a bicycle.

Walking alone, he thinks about his grandfather, and thinking about him is chilling because "his grandfather was the only person in the world to whom Figgy was tied." The possible impending loss of his grandfather makes Figgy "suddenly chilly." Although Byars does not say so, Figgy's becoming "suddenly chilly" is not because the weather has changed (it is summer) but from his fear of losing his "one tie" (*Goat*, 56). Indirectly, the change in his grandfather and his resulting strange behavior leads to Figgy's breaking his leg, certainly painful and frightening for Figgy, not only because a broken leg is painful and frightening but also because Figgy is afraid of nurses and physicians.

A casual reader of *After the Goat Man* may conclude that the story is Figgy's because he and his grandfather and their trouble generate the action and keep it moving. A closer reading, however, reveals that the story is really about Harold more than it is about Figgy and the Goat Man. Ultimately, Harold is the center of the story. Overweight and self-conscious about being fat, insecure and timid, sensitive and compassionate, and always funny, Harold V. Coleman is the most fully developed character in *After the Goat Man*.

Harold's insecurity and self-consciousness come mainly from his being overweight. He likes to eat; food is irresistible. After playing Monopoly for a day and a half with Ada and Figgy, Harold wants to stop playing and go home for supper. Because Figgy wants desperately to keep playing, he points out that it is only three o'clock: "Harold thought it could not possibly be only three o'clock. He was starving. He had been imagining that at this moment his mother was putting bowls of food on the table. He thought he had actually smelled fried potatoes" (*Goat*, 18).

Harold's self-consciousness stems in part from his being unathletic. Harold's lack of athletic ability Byars demonstrates through his inability to ride a bicycle well: "Harold was self-conscious about his slowness at anything athletic" (*Goat*, 50). Riding his ten-speed bicycle, "Harold always kept his bicycle in the lowest gear because it was easiest to pedal. The only time he got his bicycle in a higher gear was when his knee accidentally struck the gear shift" (*Goat*, 63). Harold "was conscious of the way he looked, like a demonstration of how *not* to ride a bicycle" (*Goat*, 69).

Harold's self-consciousness is inextricably connected to his insecurity. At the Dairy Queen, Ada says she wants only a small cone. Shocked, Harold asks if she does not want a Fiesta, "the grandest thing this Dairy Queen had to offer. They put every single thing they had on it." Ada says, "Nobody but goops get those." Self-conscious and insecure, "he hesitated. He could have wept" (*Goat*, 35). He orders a cone, too, although he had planned to order a Fiesta.

Harold's insecurity and timidity are reflected in his thinking "of himself and the rest of the world as a great fraction—1/3,348,000,000" (*Goat*, 87–88) and in his not wanting to go to Mr. Gryshevich's cabin by himself. When he suggests that he go for Figgy's grandfather after the accident, he hopes Ada will say, "No, you can't go by yourself" (*Goat*, 97). But she does not.

Perhaps because of his own insecurities and vulnerabilities, Harold is sensitive and compassionate despite his insensitivity to Mr. Gryshevich's having to leave his cabin and land. When he tells Figgy that his grandfather has gone back to the cabin and locked himself in, he is afraid he has hurt Figgy. Somewhat bluntly, he says, " 'Well, your grandfather has gone back to your old house, that's all, and he's locked himself in.' Harold looked at Ada because he wanted to see if she thought he had told it as badly as he did" (*Goat*, 47).

Harold's sensitivity is exhibited several times in the novel; in one of the best he humorously relates to Ada in a flashback about his Christmas gift when the poorest boy in the class got his name and gave him a dime wrapped in notebook paper. Although Harold is saddened and disappointed, he does not let on. When he sees Bubba Joe watching him, he says, "Hey, you guys, look what I got—cash" (*Goat*, 123).

Although these traits may make Harold sound sappy, he is not because Byars endows his character with the saving grace of humor. Harold has decided and then dropped a number of possible vocations, including becoming an astronaut because he might make a fool of himself on the moon. One day at the pool, he climbs up on the high diving board "mainly to see what the view was like from up there and he had not intended to jump off at all." Kids lined up behind him. The children demand that he jump. Harold "did not get to see the impact, of course, but everyone who did see it said there had never been such a splash since the pool had opened in 1960. People standing ten feet away got drenched. . . . [I]t came to him that he had better not count on being an astronaut any more. . . . [H]e saw himself landing flat on his back and sinking deep into the moon dust. The only thing TV viewers would be able to see would be a Harold V. Coleman–shaped hole in the moon's surface, like a weird crater" (*Goat*, 42–43).

Although Harold V. Coleman does not realize nor fully understand it, the new highway and its unhappy effect on the Goat Man and Figgy affect him, too; the change and upheaval affect Harold quite differently, but its effect is beneficial. Change is not something to get upset about for Harold, who changes his possible career choices more frequently than the moon waxes and wanes. Harold cannot understand all the fuss over the Goat Man, the highway and its displacing people. He "was puzzled. He did not understand why the Goat Man was making such a fuss. People had to move all the time. Jobs changed. Highways changed. You had to be ready to change too. It was the way life was" (*Goat*, 73).

At the end of the novel, Harold has changed, and for the better, although he does not understand how or why. Harold may not understand, but he has gained considerable insight into himself and has come to an understanding about his relation to humanity—that no matter how disparate we are, we are all human beings; we have our common bond of humanity. After Ada's father, Dr. Harrison, comes home from the hospital and tells Ada and Harold that Figgy is all right and has gone home with his grandfather, he says he will try to help Mr. Gryshevich find a farm. Harold pictures "the five of them—Dr. Harrison, Ada, Figgy, the Goat Man, and himself—piling into the car together. To people who didn't know them, they would look like a strange group, Harold thought, and yet they were linked together like a chain" (*Goat*, 125).

As he goes up to bed that night, he thinks to himself, "It was going to be a long time, he thought, before he understood this day. It was not

like any other day in his life. It had been a day special enough to be cel-
ebrated each year. New Year's Day. Columbus Day. Goat Man Day"
(*Goat*, 126).

If Harold is the most fully developed character in *After the Goat Man*,
then Figgy is the most appealing. He is one of those naive and vulnerable children Byars skillfully creates. Byars makes his vulnerability especially poignant with the rabbit's foot he wears on a string around his
neck as a good luck piece; it makes him feel protected. When a dog
starts barking at him, Figgy "took his rabbit's foot quickly in his hand
and said, 'It's all right. It's just me—Figgy.' Because of the rabbit's foot,
he didn't have any fear. 'This rabbit's foot really works,' he told everybody. 'You should get one.' But nobody seemed impressed. He waited,
rabbit's foot in hand, and after a moment the dog went back and lay
down by the steps. Figgy glanced around to see if anyone had witnessed
the magic. He was alone" (*Goat*, 21–22).

The rabbit's foot is Figgy's talisman to keep him from harm, but it
does not work. Just before Harold loses control of his bicycle and he and
Figgy crash to the pavement, Figgy "grabbed his rabbit's foot and held
it tightly against his chest." The bicycle skids on the pavement, and
Figgy "held his rabbit's foot tighter and shut his eyes" (*Goat*, 82). The
first thing Figgy asks for after he breaks his leg is his good luck piece;
Harold tells him it is in his hand and reaches down and closes his fingers
around it: "Figgy sighed as he felt the soft fur" (*Goat*, 93). Although the
rabbit's foot does not keep Figgy and Harold from wrecking, Figgy's
faith in the rabbit's foot is not lessened; it is a comfort to him because it
is about the only certainty he has, poignantly emphasizing his vulnerability.

Figgy's vulnerability is nowhere better expressed than in his concern
about his grandfather and his feeling that the security of his life with his
grandfather is lost because his grandfather has taken his shotgun and
gone back to his cabin. After confessing to Ada and Harold that his
grandfather is the Goat Man, he leaves them, believing he will never see
Harold and Ada again. His deep despondency Byars makes clear as he
recalls trying to make Ada laugh the way Harold can: "He felt now that
it would never happen. He would never sit on Ada's porch again and
play Monopoly. He would never get to speak into Harold's tape recorder.
He would never get to drink out of the crystal sugar bowl. He would
never make Ada laugh" (*Goat*, 59).

Before Figgy wandered up onto the Harrisons' porch, a mile from his
new home, he had never played Monopoly, "had not even known such a

game existed" (*Goat*, 16), and yet he becomes addicted to the game. He regrets Harold and Ada's decision to stop playing, and he begins neatly putting the game back into its box. Ada tells him to "stuff it back in," but his natural predilection for neatness makes him want to put it back right just as his longing for order makes him admire the clean, washed look of the "green and trimmed" yards he passes through on his way to and from Ada's house (*Goat*, 21). At Ada's he drinks from a crystal sugar bowl, and when he gets home, he looks for something similar to drink his Fizzy from, showing he likes pretty things. Figgy's clothes and body may be dirty, but he's neat. His appreciation of neatness, order, and beauty is striking and reinforces his naïveté and vulnerability. Just as his grandfather dislikes having to live in the project house, Figgy likes the house with its running water, central heat, and new appliances.

Figgy's sense of isolation adds to his vulnerability. Figgy's mother is dead, and no one knows where his father is. Although he has an Aunt Bena in Michigan or Minnesota (he cannot remember which), his grandfather is really his only relative. Figgy's relationship with his grandfather has become tenuous in the two years before the story opens and more tenuous since their move to the housing project. Depressed as he walks alone toward the cabin and his grandfather, Figgy feels cut off from the world: "Figgy sometimes thought of other people as being all wound together as if they were caught in one huge spider web. He had only one tie, like a rowboat, and that was to his grandfather" (*Goat*, 56).

Despite his vulnerability and naïveté, Figgy has a tough determination about him, evinced in his going to help his grandfather when his past efforts to help him have come to nothing. It also comes through in his wanting to play Monopoly with Ada and Harold, two people he has never seen before; and while the game leaves him greatly in debt with only a few dollars left, he is determined to keep playing if Harold and Ada will.

Figgy's vulnerability, his relationship with his grandfather, and his grandfather's anger about the change and upheaval in his life give *After the Goat Man* its strong emotional undercurrent.

Ada Harrison is the least affected by the change and upheaval in Figgy and the Goat Man's lives. She is no different in the end than in the beginning of the story. She exudes confidence. She is not afraid of anything; she is imaginative enough to make a gerbil funeral a colorful affair; she shows compassion in her concern for Figgy and his grandfather; she is a strong character and, unlike indecisive Harold and confused Figgy, makes up her mind and acts. It is she who knows instinctively what to do after the accident, and it is she who determines that she and Harold should go with Figgy to Mr. Gryshevich's cabin after his grandfather has gone there with his gun.

In addition to her use of action, dialogue, and anecdote to reveal character, Byars also uses "tags" of habitual action to give further dimension to her characters. Ada frequently puts her hair behind her ears. Figgy has his rabbit's foot and his fondness of drinking from pretty and unusual vessels—a crystal sugar bowl at Ada's and a cracked blue pitcher at home. Harold thinks about food.

Even the names of the three children suggest something about them and their personalities. Harold is not just Harold, but Harold V. Coleman, a man-sized name for a man-sized child. "Ada Harrison" is a no nonsense name, the name of a woman headed for the bench of the Supreme Court or that of an effective and proper headmistress or that of a practical and decisive physician, which she claims she will be. Figgy's name is the best of all, reflecting his personality and size. He is a fig made diminutive by adding "y," appropriate for his "bright black eyes" and small skinny body, his naïveté and vulnerability. Figs grow in the shadow of giant fig leaves, and Figgy exists in the shadow of his giant of a grandfather. When figs are ripe and eaten fresh, they have a special flavor all their own, just as Figgy does. Figgy is special. And so is *After the Goat Man*.

The Pinballs

The Pinballs (1977) is one of the most memorable and moving stories about child abuse since Bette Greene's *Summer of My German Solider* (1973) or Irene Hunt's *The Lottery Rose* (1976). Byars presents not one but three abused children coming together with Collin and Ramona Mason, foster parents, who are among the gentlest and kindest parents, foster or biological, in the Byars canon. Most writers would be satisfied to write a good story about one abused child. One can hardly read this book without laughing and crying at the same time. *The Pinballs* is bitter, sweet, sad, and funny, drawing from readers empathy, anger, pain, and pleasure—as few novels for children do.

In a nutshell, *The Pinballs* is about physical and emotional child abuse. The ways these three children—and thousands of others—are treated is enough to make one want to abolish parenthood or to take ax handles to abusive parents as Carrie Nation took axes to saloons. Because of circumstances in their pasts, the children of *The Pinballs* are emotionally stunted. Like inanimate pinballs, Thomas J, Carlie, and Harvey are thrown together in the home of kind and understanding foster parents.

Each is a foster child for very different reasons: the authorities discover eight-year-old Thomas J when his two self-appointed guardians, the 88-year-old Benson twins, Thomas and Jefferson (they are women),[8] fall simultaneously, one breaking a right hip, the other a left. Carlie's second stepfather hits her so hard that he gives her a concussion (before she passes out she whams him with a double boiler).[9] Harvey goes to the Masons because his father, in a drunken pique, accidentally puts the transmission into drive instead of reverse and runs his car over Harvey, breaking both his legs. If such ill treatment of children did not occur with frequency, readers would have to believe that Byars had lost her reason or was writing a fantasy set on another planet.

Thomas J's six years with the Benson twins have made him different from other children and a social misfit. The twins never showed Thomas J any affection except once when they patted him on his head and back when he found their father's gold watch. As a result of his six years with Thomas and Jefferson, Thomas J is starved for affection. Despite their not showing affection, ironically, Thomas J loves them, but because he has never seen affection demonstrated, he does not know how to show it.

That they took him in and cared for him in their elderly, bumbling, and absentminded fashion shows that the twins possess some human decency; they did not physically abuse him, but abuse comes in all forms. They took him in when he was left at their farmhouse "like an unwanted puppy. . . . The twins had meant to take him into town and tell the authorities, but they had kept putting it off. First it was because he was pleasant company, later because he was good help in the garden."[10]

As Thomas J and Mr. Mason drive to the hospital a second time to visit Thomas, the surviving twin, and to attend a little later the funeral of Jefferson, Thomas J confesses that he wants to say something to Miss Benson, but cannot. He wants to tell her he loves her, but he does not know how. Mr. Mason understands all too well and tells Thomas J about his visit to his mother as she lay dying and could not tell her he loved her because she had never said she loved him and had never shown him affection. Thomas J and Mr. Mason's dialogue reflects or explains in part the reasons for Thomas J's lack of social skills and why he feels unloved and cannot express his love for the twins. Mr. Mason explains,

> "Now [my mother] was a good woman, real good, but she was never one to show affection."

"The twins were like that."

"I can never remember my mother hugging me or kissing me, not one time."

"I can't remember the twins doing that to me either. They patted me one time. . . ."

"The word 'love' was never mentioned in our house that I can remember."

"Mine either. . . ."

"The word love had never been said to me in my whole life."

"Mine either."

"I mean, I know she loved me—I guess she did anyway—she took good care of me and I must have loved her, but I'd never said the word in my life."

"I haven't either." (*Pinballs*, 88–89)

Another indication that the twins showed little affection is that Thomas J can recall only three gifts they gave him: pencils with his name on them, a pair of gloves, and *Big Bible Stories for Little People*; as might be obviously expected, his favorite story is about Baby Moses: "When he heard that story he always imagined his own mother waiting by the road, hiding in the poplar trees, waiting to see the twins take him in" (*Pinballs*, 62).

Thomas J has other difficulties. Because the twins hardly ever speak, Thomas J lacks conversational skills: "Sometimes their entire daily speech was 'Water's boiling,' and 'Cronkite's on,' and 'I'm turning in' "(*Pinballs*, 61). Because the twins were rather deaf, Thomas J shouts when he talks the first few hours he is in the Mason house. Thomas J's difficulties are compounded by the Benson twins' hospitalization and their deaths. The first time he and Mr. Mason go to the hospital "he had a dread about it" (*Pinballs*, 49).

Carlie asks him why he does not take them some candy, and he points out that they do not believe in candy, chewing gum, or soda pop. The twins may well have been right in not believing in candy, gum, and pop, but their disbelief is a brilliant stroke, paradoxically reflecting both the neglect and lack of affection and care Thomas J has suffered in his six years with them; in this time they have given him the same kind of care they would give one of their farm animals, making him a social misfit. The Benson twins have abused Thomas J emotionally, but his own parents are directly responsible.

After he and Mr. Mason leave the hospital, they go to the Bensons' farm. The visit magnifies Thomas J's sense of loss: "It gave Thomas J a sad feeling to go in the Bensons' house. It seemed emptier than a house without any furniture" (*Pinballs*, 55). And the garden, which the twins had tended with care and dedication, has dried up because there has been no rain for three weeks.

Carlie has been physically and emotionally abused. Carlie's father abandoned her and her mother before Carlie was born. Her mother has married twice after Carlie's father abandoned her, and both stepfathers, especially her present one, have been abusive. Carlie says to Harvey, "You're always hearing about how dangerous the streets are and how you're going to get mugged or hit on the head? Well, in the streets I was perfectly safe. It was when I got home that I got mugged and attacked" (*Pinballs*, 65).

Physical abuse, however, is not all that Carlie has suffered from. Her mother has been able to marry three times but has never been able to marry a man who does not abuse Carlie, including her biological father, whose abuse, though not physical, is abusive as Carlie sees it. He "didn't even wait to see if I was a boy or a girl! He doesn't even know I'm *me!*" (*Pinballs*, 66). Carlie writes to her mother from the Masons, pleading for her to let her come home, but she never hears from her mother; this tells Carlie loud and clear that her mother does not care about her.

As a result of a lifetime of emotional and physical abuse, Carlie is angry and acrimonious and verbally abusive to Mrs. Mason and the two boys when the children first come to the Mason house. Carlie's upbringing, however, has not only made her defensive and rude but also has made her tough—"as hard to crack as a coconut" or a pinball (*Pinballs*, 5). Her verbal abuse of others, in the form of abrupt candor and frankness, shows a bright, intelligent young girl behind her tough facade, and despite her cruel candor, she is funny. When Harvey tells her he broke his legs playing football, she does not believe him and asks what position he played. He says, " 'Quarterback. . . .' Carlie snorted. 'You're no quarterback. . . . If you were playing football at all, you were probably the ball' " (*Pinballs*, 12). As the story progresses, however, Carlie's insulting taunts become less acrimonious, then funnier, and finally gentler and more caring, revealing a changed heart.

The most severely abused of the three children—or the one who feels his mother's abandonment and his father's rejection the deepest—is Harvey. Both Harvey's parents have abused him, his mother having left him and his father to "find" herself on a commune in Virginia; his father had not wanted a child, as Harvey learns when he overhears an argument between his parents just before his mother leaves. Harvey's mother's leaving and his father's ignoring him cause Harvey's depression. Harvey's father had promised to attend the school ceremony at which Harvey is to receive an award. Because his father wants to get to the Elks Club, he refuses. Harvey asks him to take him to the building, but his father even refuses to drop him off at the school because he's late; he shouts at Harvey to get out of the car, then pushes Harvey out, locks the door, puts his car in forward gear, and while Harvey runs around in front of the car to the unlocked driver's door, he drives over Harvey, breaking both legs.

Harvey's worst blow comes later, after he has gone to the Masons. His father comes to take him to supper and convinces him that his mother has never written to either of them, has never even answered his father's letters about Harvey's appendectomy or his bout with measles. Harvey has always thought that his mother had written him and that his father had torn the letters up. To the father's credit, however, he does not tell Harvey until Harvey forces the issue.

Harvey's depression becomes deeper after he learns his mother has never written to him. Returning from the restaurant, Harvey confesses to Carlie that he does not think he "can make it." She thinks he means he cannot make it to his bed, and when he explains what he means, Carlie realizes how deep his depression is. Harvey does not eat, and Carlie describes his condition as nearly hopeless when she says, "You know, if they made a target of him—. . . well, nobody could shoot it. . . . He looks like he's already been shot" (*Pinballs*, 96). Having grown fond of Harvey in their weeks together, Carlie becomes angry about Harvey's father, but she determines to help Harvey out of his depression. The next morning Harvey does not get out of bed, and Carlie discovers that the toes on his right foot are red and swollen from an infection in his right leg, forcing Harvey back to the hospital, where his emotional and physical conditions worsen.

With only a few pages left, a reader naturally wonders how Byars will resolve this new problem and other problems of the children; there is obviously not enough space left to bring about a resolution for the three, though both Carlie and Thomas J have made apparent progress toward healing. It's like watching a mystery. There are only five minutes left, and not a hint as to who committed the crime because all obvious suspects have been eliminated.

With help from Thomas J, Carlie comes up with a tenuous plan to help Harvey out of his severe depression. The tenuous—and suspenseful—plan works.

The resolution of Harvey's depression is delightful. Still, it is not an artificial one. Consistent with the action and characters of the story, the resolution rises naturally out of the characters and action and is consistent with Byars's plot patterns where young protagonists frequently resolve their problems without much help from adults. Carlie and Thomas J's slipping Harvey a puppy into the hospital for his birthday, the dog he has always wanted but his parents never gave him, brings Harvey out of his deep depression. Dogs have often been used in children's wards and in homes for the elderly to help alleviate depression.[11]

This potentially bleak and depressing story Byars makes palatable and more delightful with graceful, charming wit and humor. Carlie is the funniest character with the funniest dialogue. At first her acrimonious thrusts are intended to hurt or to insult; later, however, they become less painful and more humorous. The first time she sees Mrs. Mason standing in the door with her apron on to welcome her and the social worker: "'I knew she'd have on an apron,' Carlie said to the social worker. 'She's trying to copy herself after Mrs. Walton—unsuccessfully, I might add. . . . I'm not fooled by things like aprons'" (*Pinballs*, 9). Mrs. Mason tells her that she will have to stay with her until Carlie's " 'home situation stabilizes.'. . . 'Whoo,' Carlie said, 'that means I'll stay until I'm ready for the old folks home'" (*Pinballs*, 6). Mrs. Mason tells her that Harvey is coming that day and has two broken legs. " 'Well,' Carlie said, 'that lets out dancing'" (*Pinballs*, 11). Carlie tells Thomas J about the ad in the paper for puppies "free to good homes." Thomas J wants to know if the Masons' home is a good one. Carlie replies with quick insight, "If it's good enough for us, it's good enough for a dog, isn't it?" (*Pinballs*, 115).

Carlie gives physicians a hard jab while she and Thomas J are slipping the puppy into the hospital; she warns him to keep an eye out for nurses because "they are known for their sharp eyes. Doctors aren't. We could bring an elephant in here and the doctors wouldn't notice" (*Pinballs*, 117). Harvey wants to know if he can keep the puppy "permanently," and Carlie replies, "Sure, what kind of gifts do you think me and Thomas J give? If we'd wanted to give you something unpermanent we'd have gotten a Popsicle" (*Pinballs*, 119). When Carlie learns that Harvey's father has visited him in the hospital, it makes her so angry that she equates him with disease: "You mean they let that rotten bum come in Harvey's room? . . . Whoo, next thing you know they'll be letting germs and viruses in" (*Pinballs*, 113).

Carlie is bright; she is older and more experienced than Harvey or Thomas J; and she speaks—sometimes bitterly, sometimes wryly and humorously, but always with candor and intelligence—about the mistreatment of and utter disregard for children that some parents and other adults show. For a long time Harvey has wanted a puppy; he and his mother check the ads every night in the paper, and she promises him a puppy for his upcoming birthday. But she leaves for the commune a few days before his birthday, so he does not get a puppy. When he tells Carlie about his disappointment, he also tells her about the 27 pet guinea pigs his mother had when she was a little girl: "She wanted to sell them to make money, but she couldn't bring herself to part with them." It takes Carlie only an instant to see the irony in Harvey's mother's behavior and leads her to exclaim, "Whoo, that tells you something about people, doesn't it? They can't stand to part with stinking guinea pigs, but they throw their kids around like straws" (*Pinballs*, 60).

Not all the humor comes from Carlie; on their way to visit one of the Benson sisters, Mr. Mason tells Thomas J a story about the time he accidentally kicked the coffin his father's friend was lying dead in: "Mr. Joe's mouth came open. I never will forget that. I ran all the way home—seventeen blocks—hid under the bed" (*Pinballs*, 87–88).

The disregard and lack of care some adults show in having children in the first place and in their terrible treatment of them later Carlie describes in an apt and bitter simile where she sees Harvey, Thomas J, and herself as pinballs. Carlie's simile serves as an explicit statement of the central theme of *The Pinballs*. She tells Mrs. Mason, "Harvey and me and Thomas J are just like pinballs. Somebody put in a dime and punched a button and out we came, ready or not, and settled in the same groove. . . . They're just things. They hit this bumper, they go over here. They hit that light, they go over there. . . . As soon as they get settled, somebody comes along and puts in another dime and off they go again" (*Pinballs*, 29–30).

Because of her helping Harvey get over his depression and on the road to recovery, because of the kindness and patience of Mr. and Mrs. Mason, and because she has reached a new level of maturity, Carlie, by the end of the novel, no longer thinks of herself, Thomas J, and Harvey as pinballs. Although the emotional outlook of the three children has changed, their situations have altered very little.

The Pinballs is consistent with several of Byars's plot patterns where child protagonists frequently resolve their problems with or without help from adults, although the resolution of *The Pinballs* takes a somewhat different twist. While the children resolve their most immediate conflicts and find that they have the inner strength and courage similar to others of Byars's child protagonists, and although the story ends on a relatively light note, Byars offers no pat solution, no deus ex machina, to the horrors these children have already faced and have yet to face. But, happily, they have the inborn grace, intelligence, and determination to face with fortitude whatever life may hand them. At the end of the novel, Carlie tells Thomas J, "Pinballs can't help what happens to them and you and me can" (*Pinballs*, 136). It may be that Byars's greatest gift to her young readers is not, finally, just good stories to read but the hope that, with the help of kind and caring adults and with their own spiritual and emotional strength and intelligence, young people, like the heroes and heroines of fairy tales, can endure and achieve a sense of belonging, of competence, of safeness in an unsafe world—that they can love and be loved in return.

The Night Swimmers

The Night Swimmers is about sibling rivalry, jealousy, and parental neglect, but with a difference because Retta Anderson, the protagonist, is an ersatz mother for her two younger brothers, nine-year-old Johnny and preschooler Roy. In her role as a substitute mother, Retta controls Johnny and Roy, but that is where the rub comes; she is losing control of Johnny, and Roy is following his lead. Retta's role as mother and her pleasure in their dependency on her are crumbling. Retta is also jealous of Johnny and his new friend Arthur because Johnny wants to do things with him instead of with her and Roy; Retta becomes angry and hurt at the breaking up of the triumvirate of the "night swimmers."

The Night Swimmers, like many of Byars's stories, is also about a step in the growing-up process; all three Anderson children take a step toward maturity during the course of the novel. From the opening paragraph, where the three children are swimming late at night in Colonel Roberts's pool uninvited and by themselves, *The Night Swimmers* is dark and suspenseful, giving a foreboding sense of possible tragedy. Much of the story takes place at night, further adding to its dark and foreboding undertones.

The mother of the Anderson children died in a plane crash two years before the story opens; their father, Shorty, a two-bit country singer, guitarist, and songwriter working at the Downtown Hoedown (a parody of the Grand Ole Opry), is so caught up in his career that he has no time for and little interest in his three children. Shorty Anderson leaves his children to their own resources, with Retta mothering, cooking, washing, cleaning, and planning their amusements. The family has recently moved to a new neighborhood, and Retta has discovered Colonel and Mrs. Roberts's pool and a way to climb over a fence to get in. Until Retta buys swimsuits for them, the children go swimming in their underwear after the Robertses go to bed. One night, someone spies on them, and on another night, Johnny makes a lot of noise, bringing Colonel Roberts out to find the children scrambling madly to escape. Some nights later, in defiance and spite, Johnny slips out to go with his new friend Arthur to launch a hot-air balloon they have rigged with a plastic garment bag and candles. Retta follows Johnny and Arthur to a vacant lot on a hill and accosts Johnny just after they launch their balloon. Angry and jealous of Johnny's new friend, his new independence, and her loss of control, Retta stridently scolds Johnny, hurting and embarrassing him.

Meanwhile, waking up and finding Johnny and Retta gone, Roy decides they are swimming. Still in his pajamas and wanting sweet revenge for their not including him, he goes to the Robertses' pool, and in the hotness of his dream for revenge, jumps into the pool to realize only too late that they are not there. Roy cannot swim and would have drowned if Colonel Roberts had not heard his yells and rescued him in time. Colonel Roberts takes him home and calls Shorty. Before Shorty arrives, however, Retta, Johnny, and Arthur come from the balloon launch to find Colonel Roberts in the living room with Roy asleep on the sofa.

Shorty arrives and learns that his children have been swimming at night in Colonel Roberts's pool without his knowledge. Shorty's girl-friend, Brendelle, comes a few minutes later; after a a little while Colonel Roberts and Arthur leave, and Johnny and Roy go to bed. Brendelle comforts Retta, who comforts Roy and symbolically lets go of Johnny before going to bed herself.

The Night Swimmers seems more an exemplum for parents than a book for children because one of its central themes concerns a problem of many parents: how much and how long to control their children. It is not, however, Shorty who is concerned about control, but Retta. While it is true that children often feel pain and feel let down when a sibling marries, goes away to college, or leaves home for whatever reason, it is rare for a child to exercise the kind of control that Retta does over

Johnny and Roy. Because Retta's acting as a substitute mother and being in control is an unusual experience for a young sibling, this central concern of the novel makes it less universal than Byars's other major novels.

Though its subject matter dealing with controlling and letting go may make it less universal, David Rees calls *The Night Swimmers* a "somber and powerful achievement" (Rees, 45), deservedly high praise for Byars's eighteenth published book.[12] A major cause for the novel's somberness is that Retta is not an appealing protagonist. Byars's protagonists generally engage readers' sympathies, making them appealing, however flawed they may be. But Retta hardly ever arouses sympathy or appeal because she is domineering, jealous, and spiteful. Humor in Byars's novels often centers on and comes from the central character, making him or her more appealing, but in *The Night Swimmers* Retta is bossy, superior, and conceited but rarely, if ever, funny.

Retta has been forced into her role as mother by her mother's death and her father's ineffectual parenting; however, Retta herself is partly responsible for her role. She sees herself as a mother and enjoys making this role a domineering one. In a subtle jibe at television, Byars implies that Retta's role models are mothers on television soap operas and dramas.

Retta's domination of the two boys is clear from the start, and several incidents illustrate both her lack of humor and her domination. The first time the children go into the Robertses' pool, a light goes on in the house. Retta insists that the light is coming from a bathroom. When Roy asks her how she knows its coming from a bathroom, Retta haughtily and smugly replies, "I *know*. If you'd shut up, you could probably hear the toilet flush."[13] The light goes out, and although the boys are scared and cold and want to go home, Retta says they will make one more lap around the pool, which they do. Retta is a determined and hard-headed young girl: "Even if the colonel had appeared in person and had yelled at them in a military voice, she felt she would still insist that they make this one extra lap" (*Swimmers*, 7). At home after their swim Retta's domineering mothering becomes clearer when Johnny turns on the television set to watch "The Tonight Show." Retta turns it off, and with voice and body language she communicates her dominance, commanding Johnny to " 'get to bed.' She pointed with one hand to his bedroom. Her other hand was on her hip" (*Swimmers*, 9).

Retta likes her role: being in charge makes her feel good. When the children return home and Roy and Johnny are in bed, she makes a peanut butter and banana sandwich for Roy, her offer of food stemming from their successful swim together, which "made her feel more maternal than usual" (*Swimmers*, 10). She feels that she and her brothers are one against an unfair and unfriendly world. As she makes the sandwich in the kitchen, she "was happier tonight than she had been in months. She had been taking care of her brothers all her life, but this summer, since they had moved to this neighborhood, it had become a lonely task. Tonight, however, they had had fun. She and her brothers were like friends now, she decided, doing things together. The summer vacation stretched ahead as one companionable, fun-filled day after another" (*Swimmers*, 11).

As her domination makes her less appealing as a protagonist, so do her conceit and her occasional demonstration of superiority. When Johnny criticizes the way she makes spaghetti by pouring tomato soup over noodles, Retta's thoughts reveal her conceit: "Retta was never hurt by criticism of her cooking because she herself was always pleased with the results" (*Swimmers*, 29). During the first swimming episode she makes Johnny and Roy swim in the shallow end of the pool while she swims in the deep end, making Johnny defensive and rebellious. Her pride and her conceit about her swimming ability indicate her superior attitude: "She moved to the deep end and began to swim silently. She was aware that Johnny was watching her, hoping to find fault, so she moved with deliberate grace. She copied the movements she had seen the Aquamaids do on television. She turned on her back. Then she swirled and dived under the water. Her bare feet rose, toes pointed and shone in the moonlight. . . . She glanced around to see if Johnny and Roy were watching. When she was sure they were, she skinned the cat and dropped into the water without a sound" (*Swimmers*, 3).

Retta is also a jealous sibling—jealous of Johnny's developing independence and friendship with Arthur and of Roy's sometime desertion of her as his mentor and provider of amusement. Retta's brooding only adds to the novel's dispirited mood. A few nights later, when Johnny slips out and she follows him to Arthur's house and then follows both to a vacant lot, Retta senses that Johnny is happy and excited about his and Arthur's adventure, intensifying her jealousy and making her vindictive: "Every move, every word, made Retta angrier, and the more excited Johnny became, the more Retta wanted to ruin that excitement. It was all she could do to keep from running forward, grabbing his arm, and shaking away his joy. 'I'll teach you not to slip out at night,' she would say. 'I won't have this kind of behavior!' She forgets that it was she herself who had taught him to slip out in the first place" (*Swimmers*, 101).

Just after Johnny and Arthur launch their hot-air balloon of burning candles and a plastic garment bag, Retta's seething anger and jealousy come to the fore, and she approaches Johnny and attacks him physically and verbally: "Abruptly Retta grabbed him by the upper arm and spun him around. 'What do you think you're doing?' she snapped. . . . She shook him as fiercely as an animal shakes its prey. Johnny did not struggle. He allowed himself to be shaken. Suddenly Retta wanted to make his actions look as bad as possible. She leaned forward, including Arthur in her dark glance. 'What are you trying to do?' she yelled. 'Burn down the whole city?' " (*Swimmers*, 104–5).

Retta's rare kindnesses and brief periods of consideration seem false or hypocritical in light of her treatment of Johnny and Arthur the night they send up their hot-air balloon. When she is in a good temper, she behaves benevolently and lovingly toward Roy, as she does the night she offers him a peanut butter and banana sandwich after their first swim in the Robertses' pool. A few nights later, however, this benevolent and loving attitude becomes suspect when she forces Roy, by gripping his arm until it hurts, to tell her who spied on the three one night when they swam. Byars's characterization of Retta as loving and kind one minute and cold and hard the next is a superb portrayal of a child who must take on adult responsibilities. This achievement does not, however, lessen readers' antipathy toward Retta; in fact, the achievement may increase it.

The Night Swimmers is somber not only because Retta is a relatively unappealing protagonist but also because the novel lacks much of the antidotal humor of Byars's major novels. Byars is at her best in her mixture of seriousness and comedy. Although this novel contains some humor, it has less than most of her major novels. Roy, the most appealing character, offers some humor, as do Shorty's lyrics and dress. Much of the humor connected with Roy stems from his belief that the Bowlwater plant is a living plant. "A breeze blew in the window, and Roy glanced over at the billowing curtains. A heavy sweet smell filled the room. The Bowlwater plant, Roy thought. . . . To Roy the Bowlwater plant was the most enormous bush in the world, something out of 'Jack and the Beanstalk.' Any plant that could produce such a strong, fascinating smell, a smell Roy associated with the Orient, *that* plant had to have leaves as big as bed sheets and flowers like tubas" (*Swimmers*, 20–21). Roy is overweight, and his love of food adds to his appeal as a naive and insecure little boy. He is not unlike the dough boys he makes one evening from Pillsbury refrigerator dough. His belief that the Bowlwater plant is vegetative, his love of food, and his being overweight give him appeal and charm, making him and his dependency on Retta believable and convincing.

Another aspect that gives *The Night Swimmers* its somber quality is its relative lack of the figurative language with which Byars often peppers her dialogue and exposition. It is only in this novel's climactic last few chapters that figurative language, mainly similes, is used. During the hot-air balloon episode Retta shakes Johnny "as fiercely as an animal shakes its prey" (*Swimmers*, 105), an image connoting destruction and consumption. Retta's appearance at the balloon launching "at the very moment of [Johnny's] triumph had been as shocking and sudden as that of a wicked witch" (*Swimmers*, 107). Retta's behavior toward Johnny gives him "a helpless feeling . . . as if he were a puppet" (*Swimmers*, 107), a lifeless, unfeeling thing manipulated by strings, echoed a bit later in another simile about dolls.

In a perfect and telling extended simile that conveys a sense of terror, Byars conveys Retta's feelings when the full realization of what she has done in leaving Roy alone to follow Johnny and Arthur and how she has perceived her mothering of Johnny and Roy. When Arthur, Johnny, and Retta return home from the balloon launch and find Colonel Roberts in the living room with Roy, Colonel Roberts asks who is in charge. Roy points to Retta, who feels "as bewildered as a child whose dolls have come to life and are demanding real care and attention" (*Swimmers*, 114). As Shorty comes in wearing "his hot-pink cowboy suit with the rhinestone lapels," the tears in Retta's eyes turn him into a "glittering pink circle," making him seem "to swirl away like a Frisbee" (*Swimmers*, 114). Byars's choice of words in this metaphor and this simile suggests that Shorty is more glitter than substance, a bit of pink light, colorfully swirling away from his responsibilities to his children.

Another simile describes Shorty's surprise at his learning that the children have been swimming in the Robertses' pool at night, that Retta has left Roy at home by himself, and that Roy's impulsive swim could have caused him to drown: Shorty "looked around him like a man who has just discovered the sun rising in the west" (*Swimmers*, 118). Byars's image has humor, but the humor is sublimated by the sobering horror that would come with such an event. As a father, Shorty contributes to the dark and somber tones of *The Night Swimmers* because he creates a aura of despair with his outlandish clothes, his ridiculous lyrics, and his lack of interest in his children. If the predicament of his children were not bleak, Shorty would be a funny, satirical portrait of a second-rate country music singer and composer. Even so, he does offer some humor as a parody of the male country-western singer, especially in his dress and in the songs he writes.

The night after Shorty's wife, Mavis Lynn, died in a plane crash, he wrote a song in her honor, "My Angel Went to Heaven in a DC-3." With a subtle, ironic twist, Byars has Shorty ignoring the fact that the plane went *down*, not up. During the time the song was popular, Roy was "much in demand." He wore "a black satin cowboy outfit made up for his appearances. Within another month the song went off the charts, and Shorty went back to wearing the reds and pinks and purples that he preferred" (*Swimmers*, 26).

Shorty dresses in one of his colorful outfits and eats supper just before he goes to the Downtown Hoedown: "He sat at the table and began to spread paper napkins over his purple cowboy suit to protect it from spills. It took eight napkins" (*Swimmers*, 35). Outlandish dress is, like beauty, in the eye of the beholder, but most beholders probably think Shorty's "red cowboy suit with white satin cactus plants on the yoke" on the outlandish side, at least. The night Colonel Roberts rescues Roy, Shorty comes in from the Downtown Hoedown wearing "his hot-pink velour cowboy suit with the rhinestone lapels, his favorite. . . . It cost twenty-two dollars to have it cleaned" (*Swimmers*, 87). He has pink boots to match.

After things settle down on the night of Roy's rescue and Retta's confrontation with Johnny and Arthur, Brendelle, Shorty's girlfriend, suggests he change: "One spot of mayo and that pink velour is ruined" (*Swimmers*, 123). Shorty likes his colorful clothes. Going to his room to change, he admires himself in the mirror, "having one last look at himself in his pink suit before he took it off. He turned sideways. The sight of himself in velour, a star's material, made him feel a little better" (*Swimmers*, 124). Because Shorty is vain and short, he does not want to be fat and short. And because he is short, he wears boots to make himself taller: "In his high-heeled boots he was two inches taller than his daughter; without them, an inch shorter" (*Swimmers*, 33). Shorty does not eat much, explaining to Retta that "short people can't eat like other people" (*Swimmers*, 35).

The songs Shorty writes and sings are in keeping with his style of clothing; they are on the garish side, a parody of some country and western songs. During the story he composes and records "You're Fifty Pounds Too Much Woman for Me," whose first title was "You Used to Be Too Much Woman, but Now You Ain't Enough." The song suggests that the woman has gained weight; the second stanza suggests where she's lost and gained; it is clear that Byars makes Shorty look only superficially at women. To Shorty, how they look is more important than what they really are: "Your teeth thinned down, but your lips swelled out. / Your nose got fat and your chin's a waterspout. / Your cheeks they flap, and your eyelids overlap" (*Swimmers*, 50).

Inadequate as a composer and a singer, Shorty is inadequate as a father, too. The day Retta follows Roy, Johnny, and Arthur to the park where they are flying Arthur's mechanical yellow airplane, she returns home feeling both angry and sad. At home she finds her father with his guitar. Hot, flushed, hurt, and angry, she obviously needs help, but Shorty does not notice: "It seemed that all her life, at every vital moment, Shorty Anderson had been composing a song" (*Swimmers*, 54). When she needs her father, he is always out of reach and out of touch. The night after her mother died, Retta goes to the living room to join her father, seeking comfort in her grief. Shorty is absorbed in composing a song about his wife's going to heaven in a DC-3. Shorty rebuffs her, "You can stay in here, but you have to be quiet." Retta gets no comfort from Shorty, only more pain—"the unswallowed, unspoken pain of her mother's death stayed in her throat so long that sometimes she thought she would die of it" (*Swimmers*, 54–55).

Retta, however, is not the only one to suffer from Shorty's indifference and neglect; Johnny does, too. The morning that Retta and Roy go to the mall to ride the merry-go-round, Johnny does not go with them because he is chafing under Retta's control. He goes to Shorty's room to awaken him, needing attention and counseling, but Shorty is half-asleep and half-awake, dreaming about singing "You're Fifty Pounds Too Much Woman for Me" at the Grand Ole Opry, and pays little attention to Johnny (*Swimmers*, 24–26).

Later that day Shorty realizes that something is bothering Retta, too, but he ignores her: "He knew something was making her unhappy, just as he had known that morning that Johnny was unhappy. However, he never interfered. After all, he hadn't interfered with Johnny, and now, only eight hours later, Johnny was on the porch, problems solved, happy as a bug. Besides, if he asked Retta what was wrong, she might tell him" (*Swimmers*, 35).

As laughable as Shorty's songs and dress are, both paradoxically add to the somber quality of *The Night Swimmers*, and his neglect of his children deepens its somberness. We see this in Retta's thoughts about Shorty's neglect: "Her father's goal—becoming a star, achieving a place where his voice made people laugh and cry, his clothes made people stare, where his life itself became the daydreams of ordinary people—that goal was so powerful that everything else, even his family, became a mere interruption" (*Swimmers*, 55).

Despite their sibling rivalry and their father's neglect, the three children take a small but vital step toward growing up. Retta takes her step when she gives up trying to control Johnny and Roy. Johnny's comes when he asserts his independence and slips out at night with his friend Arthur. Roy makes his step when he accepts the truth that the Bowlwater plant is a chemical plant and not a living organism.

In most of Byars's novels, the protagonists largely resolve their problems with their own inner strengths. Here, however, Retta, Johnny, and Roy lack or do not show the strength, conviction, and courage that Byars's other protagonists seem to possess in abundance. It is Arthur who first helps Retta see herself as holding on to and controlling her brothers, especially Johnny. As Retta, Johnny, and Arthur walk home from the hot-air balloon launch, Arthur asks Retta why she treats her "brothers like prisoners" (*Swimmers*, 107) and accuses her of thinking for them, too. But her moment of truth comes when when Johnny tells Colonel Roberts that she is in charge of him and Roy.

Significantly, it is Shorty's girlfriend, Brendelle, and not Shorty, who helps Retta put her problem with Roy and Johnny into perspective. In her talk with Retta after the tension-filled session with Colonel Roberts and Shorty, Brendelle admits to Retta, "When it comes to mothering I'm as green as grass. But I do know one thing—you can't hold on too tight. As soon as you start holding on so tight that somebody knows they're being held—well, then you're in trouble" (*Swimmers*, 121). It is Brendelle who tells Shorty he should take better care of his children and should marry (*Swimmers*, 119–20).

A little later Retta goes into Roy and Johnny's room. She lies down between the two boys and talks to Roy about the Bowlwater plant. Finally, Roy takes a step toward maturity when he accepts the fact that the plant is not a living organism: "A satisfied feeling came over Roy as he lay there. It was as if, by swallowing a hard truth about life as willing—this was the way he saw it—as Popeye swallows spinach, he had become stronger. 'There are no giant plants around here,' he said again, feeling better every time he confirmed the unhappy fact" (*Swimmers*, 129). As Retta leaves the boys' bed, she symbolically lets go of Johnny: "She turned over and hugged Johnny. Johnny stirred. He was drawn out of a dream in which he and Arthur, grown men, were sending rockets off to planets as yet unnamed. He squirmed with irritation and said, 'Let go of me.' 'I have,' Retta said" (*Swimmers*, 129).

While *The Night Swimmers* is a rather dark novel, it has its lighter aspects, and one of them is Byars's portrayal of Brendelle, Shorty's girl-friend, a clogger at the Downtown Hoedown. Although her appearances in the novel are brief, Brendelle is characterized mainly through what she says and how she says it. Brendelle is friendly and companionable with Retta; she gives Roy the kinds of hugs he really likes and enjoys. She is chatty, able to talk with the children and with Shorty. She fits right in with the family. Byars creates or captures the cadence of the speech of a woman of Brendelle's social, regional, and educational back-ground. One can almost hear her dropping her "g's" and her chatty tone when she talks to Retta, and she sometimes says "it don't."

Byars's portrayal of Brendelle is what one might expect of a hanger-on in the minor country-western music scene. She does not disguise the fact that she likes Shorty and his children, and she half-jokingly and half-earnestly suggests that she is the one Shorty should marry. It is fairly clear at the end of the novel that she and Shorty will marry. She consoles Retta, and she talks to Shorty as if they were already married, telling him to change his favorite hot-pink velour suit, "Now you go take off that suit and I'll fix you a sandwich. What kind do you want" (*Swimmers*, 123). She takes charge, telling Retta to get to bed and to sleep late the next morning, adding, "Somebody's got to start giving orders around here" (*Swimmers*, 24).

The Night Swimmers is also story about change. Retta gives up her control of Roy and Johnny; Johnny develops a friendship with Arthur and demands and receives a certain amount of independence; Roy gives up his childish belief in the Bowlwater plant as a living organism. The realization of the change in her life comes to Retta near the end of the story, just as she's going to bed: "Retta had a funny feeling. Everything had changed and yet nothing had changed. It was like those stories where a person is whisked away to a different time zone, lives a whole different life, and then returns to find that no time has elapsed at all, that everyone is still in exactly the same place" (*Swimmers*, 126). And even if everyone is in the same place and little seems changed, the major change is the most important of all: Retta's new perception of herself, her brothers, and her father. Byars seems to make clear, however, that Shorty has not changed and will perhaps never change.

The evening's events have weighed heavily on Shorty. For a brief time he recognizes his inadequacies as a father; at the same time, he feels sorry for himself. He feels so down that he cannot write a song about what has happened to him: "It seemed to him that every time his life started getting good, something bad happened. His song, 'You're Fifty Pounds Too Much Woman for Me,' was on the charts, and now just when he wanted to devote his full time to making it a hit, the burdens of fatherhood fell upon him. It made him feel so low he didn't even want to write a song about it" (*Swimmers*, 123).

Shorty's feeling bad does not last long, however. A few minutes later, after standing in front of the mirror admiring himself dressed in his pink velour suit, he begins to feel better, "his fatigue began to ease" (*Swimmers*, 124). He tells Retta that his new song has reached 89 on the charts. She expresses her hope that it will go to the top, and Shorty feels even better, "his energy was returning" (*Swimmers*, 125). A few minutes later, Shorty is composing another song, "You Got Sixteen Kinds of Fools in Me." For Shorty, "nothing had changed." He will never change, never be the parent he should be, always the two-bit country music singer and composer, making him, of the sadness of *The Night Swimmers*, the saddest of all.

The Two-Thousand-Pound Goldfish

Though it has, perhaps, just as much humor as Byars's other novels, *The Two-Thousand-Pound Goldfish* (1982) is a depressing novel. One feels while reading it that the world is as drab as Warren finds it when he comes out of the theater after watching a monster movie three times and as drab as the apartment where he lives with his half-sister, Weezie (Louise), and his maternal grandmother. It is not, however, just the drab setting Byars creates to complement the thematic underpinning of the story that makes *The Two-Thousand-Pound Goldfish* depressing; it is also depressing because of its subject, the emotional abuse of children.

Warren Otis, the protagonist, has been handed a double dose of parental emotional abuse. His mother has deserted her two children because she has had to go into hiding as a fugitive wanted by the FBI for her part in stink bombing, pipe bombing, and Molotov cocktail attacks on various organizations. His father has also deserted him: "Warren and Weezie had different fathers. Weezie's father lived in the city and gave money for her support and was learning computer science. Warren's father lived a fugitive life like his mother and sent no money."[14]

As a result of his parents' desertion and other circumstances beyond his control, eight-year-old Warren has created two fantasies to escape his emotionally drab and depressing life: (1) the monster movies he vividly and convincingly visualizes, including characters and dialogue he creates for them, and (2) the idea that his absent mother will return and take him in her arms and love him and make his life happy.

Most of Warren's waking hours seem to be taken up with remembering his mother and wanting her to return or imagining scenarios for horror movies, especially of the one he is enthralled with at the moment: creating a movie about Bubbles, the goldfish Weezie has flushed down the toilet, growing to 2,000 pounds and "ingesting" the unwary humans who, for one reason or another, have entered the city's huge and labyrinthine sewers where Bubbles has been exposed to chemical wastes and has become enormous.

The film scenarios that the troubled and unloved Warren creates are highly imaginative and far-fetched—scenarios that he often directs and rarely puts himself into. They are Byars's means of showing how emotionally tortured Warren is by his mother's desertion, by his rather unaffectionate grandmother, and by his blunt and candid sister, Weezie, who, unknown to Warren, is as as hurt by their mother's desertion as Warren. To further emphasize the extent of Warren's emotional distortion and inability to deal with feeling unloved, Warren even has Bubbles, the giant fish, eating—"ingesting" as Warren calls it—in giant slurps not only strangers but also Weezie and his grandmother. In another scenario Warren creates Bossy, a radioactive cow who squirts her death-dealing milk on his grandmother. The imagined deaths of Weezie and his grandmother stem from their attitude toward him; neither seems to understand how hard his not having a mother is, which is made only worse by Weezie's stern directness in her dealings with Warren and by his grandmother's lack of affection.

Even so, Warren feels guilty for having his relatives die: "He felt a pang of guilt. He always did when he allowed his relatives to be the victims in his horror movies. After he had allowed Bossy to squirt radioactive milk on Grandma, he had not slept well for two nights" (*Goldfish*, 16).

Warren, however, never lets his mother die in any of his scenarios "because, of them all, his mother was the most likely to have something happen to her in real life. She had enough danger without radioactive cows and man-eating snails" (*Goldfish*, 19). Perhaps he does not have his mother die because she is so far removed from the reality of his life that she symbolizes an idealized mother who will return and solve all his difficulties and who will love him as neither Weezie nor his grandmother does.

Despite the horror of some of Warren's imagined scenarios, Byars also uses them to create humor to lessen the horror in the films and in Warren's unloving world. A giant skunk, a radioactive cow, and hospital pipes that become snapping iron rattlesnakes are funny, and for whatever reason Warren dreams up his wild scenarios, they are original, inventive, and humorous. A radioactive cow lifting her leg to squirt milk even Warren knows will induce laughter, not fear, in a movie audience. Warren's ending for his movie about Bubbles is one of the funniest scenes in the novel. As Warren follows the men and women into the sewers to kill Bubbles, a reporter sees Warren and learns how Bubbles came to be in the sewers. He interviews Warren, who wants to save Bubbles—after all, she is the victim of man's pollution—and the reporter devises a solution. He calls on every citizen to flush a toilet—which even means stopping busses so that passengers can get off to find a toilet to flush—at the same moment, creating such a flood in the sewers that the floodgates will open and Bubbles will be washed out to sea.

Although not as fully developed as Warren, Weezie is one of Byars's fine female characters, and if she appears cold, distant, and unsympathetic toward Warren, it is because, as Warren and readers do not know or realize at first, she wants and needs their mother just as much as Warren does but knows that their mother will not, cannot, ever return to them. Furthermore, Weezie sees the irony, selfishness, and incongruity of her mother's abandonment for causes that turn her into a criminal; Weezie is old enough to understand that their mother loves the causes she fights for more than she loves them.

In the spring before the book opens, Warren and Weezie's mother, Saffron (Saffee for short), spends three months in the city, and although she sees Weezie and Warren, she does not contact them, and they do not know she has been there until after she has gone. Later, while discussing with Aunt Pepper and Warren their mother's visit to town, Weezie points out that her mother forgets that she and Warren have needs as strong as, if not stronger than, her own. Aunt Pepper tells Weezie that their mother "felt better after she saw you." Impassioned, Weezie says, "And so off she goes feeling better, without a backward glance. Without once thinking that Warren and me might want to feel better too. We could use a little satisfaction ourselves. I wanted to see my mother! Warren wanted to see her! And yet the only thing that mattered to her was *her* satisfaction, *her* feelings" (*Goldfish*, 110). Weezie's pain and anger are so great that she uses "me" instead of "I" as she would normally.

Significantly, Byars has Warren present for the discussion because what he learns from Weezie will help him come to grips with his mother's not returning as he often dreams she will.

Byars carefully and slowly develops Warren's realization that his mother is never going to return; for her to make it a sudden realization would flaw *The Two-Thousand-Pound Goldfish*. In numerous scenes Byars has Warren recalling his mother and longing for her return—scenes that are painfully real, arousing sympathy for Warren and making clear why he is addicted to escaping into his imagined scenarios. Warren "wanted to be scooped up in her thin arms, spun around, kissed. That was the only thing in the world that could take away this terrible feeling of loneliness" (*Goldfish*, 28). Warren "had missed her and longed for her and wept more tears for her than anybody. . . . If he had thought it was possible [to find her] he would have been roaming the earth like a nomad" (*Goldfish*, 37).

One time when Warren thinks about his mother, he sees in his mind's eye the kind of mother he longs for. The mother he wants is so normal and so ordinary that his picture reveals how greatly he misses his mother and the common, simple, everyday things that mothers do for their children. Warren wants "one of those mothers he saw in Sky City, standing in line to have their children's pictures made, the children as clean and combed as if they'd just come out of a box. . . . He wanted a mother who cared what he got on his report card and came to school for conferences and raised a fuss when his pictures weren't up on the bulletin board. He wanted a mother who would make cupcakes for the Halloween carnival and make him go to Sunday School on Sunday and—" (*Goldfish*, 50–51).

Warren's desire and longing for his mother's return is so great that he refuses to believe she is a person not meant to be a mother, even though Weezie tries to make him understand this. Weezie points out what life with their mother was like, so preoccupied with protests that her children might as well not exist. She tells Warren,

> The old times, the good old days you want to recreate, were Mom rushing in and out of the house and you and me trying desperately to get her attention and tell her something that had happened at school or something we were worried about and her saying, "Go on, go on, I'm listening," while she painted signs and cut out pictures of injured Vietnamese and made telephone calls. That was all we ever were to Mom—a background noise, like the radio, something to listen to while she was busy

with what really interested her. The only reason she had us was because
she was anti-abortion. (*Goldfish*, 48)

A few minutes later, she tells Warren, "You are not going to like what
you find" (*Goldfish*, 51).

Although Weezie's recalling what their mother was like when she was
home and her declaration cause a crack in Warren's strong belief in his
mother's love and in her returning to care for him, Warren tries to convince himself of her love by reading late one night the few postcards that
his mother has sent. The postcards are about what his mother has been
doing with brief closings, "Remember me. Miss you" and "—laughing
and happy, and that's the way I hope you two are. Love me. Miss me"
(*Goldfish*, 54–55). Warren's belief in his mother's love is so great that he
cannot read the truth of the closings, that there is nothing about loving
him and Weezie, that they only tell of their mother's self-centeredness.

At the same time, however, Warren does have a glimpse of the truth
about his mother: "The postcards came from everywhere, it seemed,
places he wouldn't have minded visiting himself—the amusement park,
the White House. This flitting around made her seem more like a crea-
ture of nature than a mother. She was like a bird or a moth. . . . And it
did not really seem like she was saving the world. Marches and bumper
stickers didn't seem like a Wonder Woman struggle. He felt a faint stirring of guilt as this unsettling thought took root and grew" (*Goldfish*,
55–56).

Looking more closely at the cards, Warren begins to see them in a
new light; his mother makes no "mention of hardship, of loneliness.
Sure, . . . she said, 'Love you. Miss you,' but she hadn't even bothered to
make those thoughts into complete sentences. . . . He felt betrayed"
(*Goldfish*, 56).

When Warren's grandmother first goes to the hospital, Warren
thinks rather happily—as would be natural for him—that his mother
will have to come home if his grandmother dies. He imagines at his
grandmother's funeral he will see his mother disguised and some
distance away behind a tombstone. No one else sees the lone figure
behind the stone, and after the funeral as the grieving mourners leave,
Warren stays behind, and she comes to him: "there she would be—his
mother. . . . She would have taken off her hat, and her hair—the red
color he remembered—would be back from her pale face. . . . And then
his mother would hold out her arms in the way he had imagined so

often, only this time it would be really happening. And he would run forward with a glad cry, and they would—" (*Goldfish*, 87–88).

Warren's grandmother does die, and there is a funeral, but it is nothing like Warren imagined. Warren's epiphany, his discovery of the truth about his mother, comes during the funeral. The cemetery is flat, there are no tombstones for his mother to hide behind, and Warren realizes his mother "would not bother to come" (*Goldfish*, 113). But suddenly, in the distance under some trees, Warren sees a figure, a red-headed figure. He believes so strongly that it is his mother he starts to rise from his chair. When the figure turns around Warren immediately understands who he sees is one of the cemetery workmen waiting to shovel the earth into his grandmother's grave. His dream is shattered, and his disappointment is so great that he begins to sob loudly and uncontrollably, bringing sympathy and attention, but no one realizes, and he cannot tell, that he is not weeping for his grandmother but for the realization that his mother will never come.

In Warren, Byars gives a convincing picture of a pathetic child starved for affection, coming to a realization that nothing he can do or dream will bring his mother back and let him feel and know the reality of his mother's love. Often in Byars's novels, the protagonists resolve their problems from an inner kind of strength and courage that they have not hitherto perceived or realized. Warren's epiphany, his recognition of the truth, also comes from an inner strength and courage that he had not known he possessed. Perhaps Warren's courage and strength are greater than those of many of Byars's other protagonists because his belief in his mother's love for him and his hope of her returning, which Byars dramatically and convincingly demonstrates, is so strong that it takes even greater strength and courage for Warren to accept the truth than for some of Byars's other protagonists.

And, as in other novels, Warren's epiphany or recognition does not bring a closed ending. Aunt Pepper will move in with him and Weezie and redecorate the apartment. Warren is considering giving up creating monster movies, is beginning to miss his grandmother, is beginning to admire and appreciate Weezie and to transfer some of the affection he's felt for his mother to her. Still, the novel gives thoughtful readers pause because they know that Warren will carry the emotional scars of his mother's desertion with him throughout life, they know that Warren's uncontrollable tears at his grandmother's funeral did not wash away the scars. Byars is an artist and a realist. She knows and demonstrates in this and in other novels that there are no easy solutions to the problems children face in real life or in fiction.

Cracker Jackson

Cracker Jackson (1985) is a novel that cannot be put down. From the opening sentence—"There's a letter for you"—the novel builds in suspense. What readers who have ever had a letter can resist such an opening sentence? They want to know whom the letter is from and what it says. Curiosity heightens in the next few sentences because the envelope is pink with "yellow roses on its flap. [Cracker's] name and address were in pencil. There was nothing to indicate danger" (*Cracker*, 3).

Nearly all critics make critical claims, choices, and judgments about what they like or do not like about a work of art, be it a painting, a composition, or a novel; afterwards, they spend their efforts in justifying their claims, choices, and judgments based on accepted criteria, citing examples from the work of art for support. *Cracker Jackson* may likely be the best book Byars has written, including her Newbery Medal winner, *The Summer of the Swans*; while this is a rather significant claim to make about her canon, there are many reasons that this may be her best book, including its difficult and unlikely theme handled sensitively and sympathetically, its excellent characterization, its carefully crafted plot, and its judicious humor.

A primary theme of *Cracker Jackson* is that wife abuse may affect many people tragically—not only the abused, but also the abuser and those close to the abused. Using wife battering as the central topic of a children's book is risky because it is not the kind of subject that most parents and teachers want children's stories to be about and because it is inherently sensational. That many children and parents suffer because one parent, usually the mother, is abused does not mean that it will make a good subject for a children's novel; the reality is painful enough without having to experience it fictionally. Byars, however, is one writer for children who can take such a painful subject and handle it with seriousness and reality and make it bearable with humor, superb characterization, and a carefully developed plot.

Byars has three major characters in the story, Jackson "Cracker" Hunter, Ralph "Goat" McMillan, and Alma Alton. Cracker's parents are divorced. His mother works as a flight attendant, and his father lives in California. Cracker is the protagonist through whom Byars tells the story, and though no single word could characterize him, "sweet" is the one that comes closest. His former baby-sitter, Alma, has nicknamed him "Cracker" because to her "he's like a box of Cracker Jack—all sweet with surprise inside, like you know, in a box of Cracker Jack you always get a little prize or a toy or a decal you can paste on yourself? Well, that's what he reminds me of—real sweet, but always coming up with a surprise" (*Cracker*, 16–17).

Cracker is a somewhat tense young boy because he strongly believes that Alma's husband, Billy Ray, is beating her. Byars has to establish clearly and reasonably the feeling that Cracker has for Alma, or his concern for her after Billy Ray starts battering her would be unrealistic. His love for Alma hardly knows any bounds, and it is difficult to see why Cracker loves Alma as much as he does until the details about their relationship become clear under Byars's expert hands. First of all, Alma was Cracker's favorite of all his sitters. Young and somewhat like a child herself, Alma has a special feeling for him, and Cracker knows she loves him. When a person loves someone, it is easy to respond in like manner, which, of course, Cracker does. When he sees her kissing her baby, Nicole, on her brow, he recalls how she did that to him when he was smaller and how good it made him feel (*Cracker*, 21).

Before her marriage, Alma stays with Cracker while his mother is on her job as a flight attendant; she calls him pet names and wishes she could take him to Billy Ray's garage. What child can resist the conspiratorial temptations Alma offers? " 'There's tires to play in, and you could fingerpaint in the grease pan. And there's a Coke machine and a peanut machine. You put in a penny and you get a handful of peanuts. But I guess I can't. If your mother found out we went to the garage, she wouldn't let me come back.' She had to say it several times before Jackson caught on. Finally he said what Alma was waiting to hear: 'She won't find out' " (*Cracker*, 30–31). As a result, Alma takes him often to Billy Ray's garage, where "his first feeling of accomplishment had come from handing tools to Billy Ray" (*Cracker*, 19).

Cracker loves Alma with the total and trusting devotion that children sometimes develop for an adult outside their family. Cracker's feeling for Alma is enhanced because she does things with Cracker that give him happiness he has never known before, as the time they waded together in the creek: "He was five years old but he had never been allowed to wade before, and stomping around in the muddy water made him happier than he had known it was possible to be" (*Cracker*, 29). Another happy time he recalls is Alma's dancing with him: "He and Alma danced a lot at home when his mother wasn't there. Alma was a good dancer and they slowdanced and frugged and even tangoed, with Jackson's feet never touching the floor. His favorite was the clog" (*Cracker*, 69).

Cracker's love for Alma may also stem from her own childlike attitudes and feelings. Alma has the innocence of a child, a good and kind child, which even irrepressible Goat, Cracker's best friend, discovers when he pretends to be a collector with his sister's UNICEF materials and goes at Cracker's request to Alma's house to see if she is all right. When he returns to Cracker waiting down the street, he says, "I wish I hadn't done that—taken her money. I mean, I'm going to give it to my sister and everything, but I just wish I hadn't done it. She was so nice" (*Cracker*, 52).

After Alma marries Billy Ray and has Nicole and after Cracker suspects that Billy Ray beats Alma, Alma and Cracker's roles seem to switch, with Cracker's becoming the caretaker and Alma's becoming the cared for. Cracker is compassionate, demonstrated by his concern for Alma and Nicole, forcing him into a difficult role that few 11-year-old boys are capable of dealing with. When Alma tells Cracker on the telephone that Billy Ray has hurt Nicole, "he was overcome with sadness . . . the kind of sadness . . . that comes when the whole world goes wrong" (*Cracker*, 72). For many reasons, but mainly because of his love and compassion for Alma, Cracker makes a supreme effort to get Alma and Nicole away from Billy Ray, actually risking his, Goat, Alma, and Nicole's lives in a dangerous drive nearly to Avondale—a danger that Byars sublimates and lessens in one of the funniest scenes in the novel.

For all his good traits, however, Cracker is not a paragon of virtue. He sometimes does some of the disgusting things that all children do at one time or another. At his great-grandmother's birthday party, he licks the salt shaker. To his mother's horror, he sometimes talks with food in his mouth and uses his clothes to wipe his nose on; in nursery school had gone through a stage of spitting on people, including his teacher, Miss Peggy.

Perhaps one of the most irrepressibly delightful characters that Byars has created is Ralph "Goat" McMillan, Cracker's best friend. Goat's animal spirits and pranks furnish most of the humor in the novel, both during the present action of the story and in flashbacks. When the story opens, Mrs. McMillan has grounded Goat because he and Percy Gill with sounds of vomiting have poured wet popcorn from the balcony of the theater onto three girls below. Although Goat's high jinks may be a bit on the repulsive side at times, they are, nonetheless, funny. One time Goat had persuaded all the kids in science class to mouth their answers without sound when the teacher, Mr. Fellini, asked them questions: "That way, Goat said, Mr. Fellini would think he was going crazy and would go to the infirmary, leaving them free to have an extra recess" (*Cracker*, 46). To pay Goat's sister Rachel the money she thinks Goat took up for UNICEF but kept for himself, Goat and Cracker get jobs raking leaves. At Mrs. Marino's they seem to play as much as they work, and about every five minutes Mrs. Marino comes to the door and tells them she is not paying them "to jump up and down in leaf piles . . . [and] to put each other in leaf bags" (*Cracker*, 60–61). Each time, Goat has an answer for Mrs. Marino. Goat hides once in a large pile of leaves to scare Cracker: " 'Boys!' It was Mrs. Marino again. 'I'm not paying you to play in the leaves' " (*Cracker*, 64). Although Goat has high animal spirits, he is honest. Goat confesses they were playing and tells Mrs. Marino she can deduct the play time from their wages.

Another of Goat's distinguishing characteristics is Byars's having him use words young boys do not normally use, indicating his intelligence and natural exuberance and making him sound adult. He tells Mrs. Marino that their playing in the leaves "was just a brief moment of frivolity" (*Cracker*, 64). Recalling the time he drove the car through the back garage wall into the laundry room and "totaled the washer-dryer" (*Cracker*, 78), Goat says, "The laundry room disaster was obviously a fluke" (*Cracker*, 99). Byars can make a character come alive with only a few lines. When Cracker and Goat are talking about driving Alma and Nicole to a refuge for battered wives in Avondale, Goat says he does not know the way. Cracker tells him, "There are maps in the car." Goat's reply reveals his quick wit, his always being ready with an answer, no matter what the provocation, and what he thinks about maps: "Have you ever had a good look at a map, pal? It's just a bunch of lines. It doesn't tell you a thing" (*Cracker*, 80).

Another character that makes *Cracker Jackson* outstanding is Alma. At first glance, Alma may seem like a stereotype and a parody of a woman who has achieved the age of an adult but who acts like an adolescent. Alma, however, is much more complex than a stereotype or a parody, though she is some of both. Early in the story Byars establishes Alma as a loving person; she loves Cracker and she loves her little daughter, Nicole. The pet names she has for Cracker when she sits with him and the similar pet names she has for Nicole surely reveal, too, a loving person. But the pet names reveal as well a kind of naive sweetness, kindness, and innocence and a person with a somewhat limited ability and background. "Gumdrop," "Pop Tart," "Cupcake," "Doughnut,"

"Muffin," and "Patty Cake" are some of the names she uses, and all of them are sweet foods, although she occasionally uses other names—"Angel," "Sunshine," and "Pumpkin"—that seem to suggest Alma sees Cracker and Nicole as less than human, something more akin to her complete collection of Barbie and Ken dolls.

That Alma has named her daughter for her favorite character on the soap opera *All My Children* also reflects her limited background. Her lack of experience and her seeing children as something to be played with like dolls make more understandable her falling in love with and marrying a man of Billy Ray's nature. She is unable to perceive Billy Ray as a human being with uncontrollable emotions. Although Alma dates Billy Ray about five years before she marries him, she apparently does not really know him or see the cruel side of him. Goat sees Billy Ray only one time and decides he's dangerous and tells Cracker, "You do not want to mess with him. He's bad news. Anybody who has a python tattooed on his arm—" (*Cracker*, 13).

Further enhancing or emphasizing her naïveté and limited knowledge of the world and people's character, Alma goes to a fortune teller, Sister Rose, to learn if she will marry Billy Ray. Alma is too trusting to know that Sister Rose is smart enough to learn from Alma anything she needs to tell Alma her fortune. Alma, true to her trusting and innocent nature, pays attention to only what she wants to hear from Sister Rose—that she will marry Billy Ray, which makes her radiantly happy: "in the dim light of Sister Rose's living room, [Alma's] face shone with enough glow to brighten the whole room. [Cracker] had not known it was possible for a person to be that happy" (*Cracker*, 69). Alma may have said something about Billy Ray that makes Sister Rose suspect he is mean, because she tells Alma just as she and Cracker are leaving that Alma will "live to regret" marrying Billy Ray.

Although Alma is not a stereotypical character, she is typical of many battered wives. She denies to Cracker that the suspicious bruises are from Billy Ray and claims they are from other causes. A black eye comes from her hitting her eye on a door. Bruises and lacerations come from a car accident she was in. Changing her mind about going to Avondale and having Cracker and Goat take her back home reflects the battered-wife syndrome of "asking for more" by not getting out of harm's way when opportunities arise.

With a firm hand and a few carefully chosen and presented details, Byars builds Alma's character as a naive and unsophisticated young woman, as reflected in the stationery she chooses (yellow roses and gardenias on the envelope flaps), in her penchant for keeping a neat and tidy house as if it were doll house with nothing out of place, in her dreaming at one time of being a flight attendant like Cracker's mother, putting on his mother's uniforms and seeing herself "flying to Chicago and San Francisco and other far places, pulling matched luggage on wheels behind her, not a hair out of place, her dark glasses set stylishly on her head" (*Cracker*, 21–22).

For all her naïveté and lack of sophistication, however, Alma can be cool and mature. After she warns Jackson to keep away from Billy Ray because she is afraid he will hurt Cracker, he goes to their house anyway. While he is there, Billy Ray drives up and stops by the porch where Alma and Nicole are swinging and talking to Cracker. Cracker ducks into the bushes at the edge of the porch, and with a nonchalance worthy of a soap opera star, Alma thinks of a way to get Billy Ray to the back yard: "I want to show you something. I've found the perfect place for Nicole's jungle gym" (*Cracker*, 27).

Alma is perhaps as close to a tragic figure as any character in Byars's novels. Her love of children and her kindness and naïveté give her the nobility of a tragic figure; ironically, it is her innocence, along with her refusal to see Billy Ray's abuse for what it is before it is too late, that make up her tragic flaw, and she falls, not just figuratively but literally to the floor after Billy Ray strikes her with a wrench. She wakes up in the hospital with "broken ribs, a punctured lung, a broken cheekbone, broken teeth, a broken wrist, and facial lacerations" (*Cracker*, 122). And a daughter with a concussion. What keeps Alma from being a tragic figure in the Aristotelian sense is that she survives—not the same, of course, but with hope, which true tragic figures never have. As Cracker sees her and talks with her the first time in the hospital, he thinks "the two halves of her face showed exactly what was going on inside her—half of her had been hurt so bad it would never be the same, but the other half still hoped for something good" (*Cracker*, 126).

Cracker Jackson is Byars's twenty-fourth published book, making her a seasoned and experienced writer, able to create highly believable and consistent characters played against each other in a story with tragic overtones. Byars's superb characterization makes the novel one of her best, but aiding in making it one of her finest novels is the plot, with its multiple threads of conflict and their reasonable and realistic resolutions. Byars understands that serious conflicts do not come to an end with everything neatly tied, that not all problems end on the final page or with the sunrise and a new day.

Children like plots neatly tied up, with nothing to worry about after the last page. These kinds of plots, however, have been fewer since the "new realism" in children's fiction of the 1960s, beginning with Louise Fitzhugh's *Harriet the Spy* (1964). Perhaps fiction before the 1960s gave children a somewhat prettified view of the world because the conflicts of those stories often had nearly perfect resolutions. Before the 1960s an open-ended novel for young readers was nearly as rare as lilies at the North Pole. Children should be permitted to be children and to enjoy childhood; at the same time, however, their fiction should not present reality with always happy endings because happy endings and totally resolved conflicts are rare in real life.

At the end of *The Great Gilly Hopkins* Katherine Paterson has Gilly's foster mother, Trotter, tell Gilly that there are no happy endings after Gilly says, "Nothing turned out the way it's supposed to." Trotter replies, "How you mean supposed to? Life ain't supposed to be nothing, 'cept maybe tough. . . . [A]ll that stuff about happy endings is lies. The only ending in this world is death. . . . [Y]ou just fool yourself if you expect good things all the time. They ain't what's regular—don't nobody owe 'em to you."[15] Although Trotter's answer may not be what children and adults want in fiction or in life, Trotter's answer is the truth. "And they lived happily ever after" is not.

Plots in realistic fiction often follow a cause-and-effect pattern; a writer of realistic fiction usually places a character in circumstances that create conflicts for the protagonist, which become a cause, or causes, leading to a particular, and sometimes predictable, effect. In a complex plot there may be many causes and many effects and the effects in turn may become causes with other effects. The protagonist in *Cracker Jackson* is Cracker, pitted against an antagonist, the batterer of his friend and former sitter, Alma, whom at one point only Cracker can help, a large order for an 11-year-old boy. Helping Alma is something that Cracker is not emotionally or physically equipped to do. Closely tied to Cracker's conflicts is Alma's conflict of coping with and surviving Billy Ray's abuse and keeping him from hurting Nicole. The causes of these conflicts are many and varied, all of which Byars presents in a series of actions taking place in the present or in the past in a series of interwoven flashbacks.

The first and major effect is that Alma must turn to Cracker for help because she has no one else. She cannot get help from her mother (who has left town six months earlier and whom she has not heard from since), from her best friend Margie (Billy Ray will force her to tell where she has gone), from the police (who will believe a contrite Billy Ray when he promises he will not beat Alma again), nor from Cracker's mother (off working as a flight attendant). Alma has not wanted Cracker's mother to know about her black eye and bruises, but in her desperation she telephones her and learns from Cracker that his mother is out of town.

This effect becomes a cause, making Cracker take his mother's car from the garage because Alma cannot drive and, with Goat's help, drive Alma to Avondale, 26 miles away, where there is a refuge for battered wives. Before they reach Avondale, however, Alma changes her mind and insists on being taken home. The effects or results of Alma's decision bring about another series of effects: Cracker's mother realizes that someone has driven her car, and just as she is about to learn who, Jackson's father telephones. In his downcast mood, Cracker does not respond as he usually does to his father's playful banter, even finds it unbearable, and for the first time since his father and mother were divorced, he hangs up on his father. Mr. Hunter calls back immediately, and both parents know that something is wrong with Cracker. Mrs. Hunter demands to know what's wrong with Cracker: "He suddenly realized that all the terrible, unspeakable pain could be put into one simple word. 'Alma,' " (*Cracker*, 104).

Mrs. Hunter intervenes and assumes the responsibility of helping Alma. But it is too late, for Alma and Mrs. Hunter do not realize that Billy Ray listens to their telephone conversation on his extension in the garage.

Cracker's conflicts are resolved not happily, not even satisfactorily, because life is not like that. Byars's resolution to Cracker's conflict with Billy Ray's abuse is logical and realistic. Byars knows that the problem is too great for an 11-year-old to handle; therefore, she devises a believable sequence of events to turn the problem over to an adult, Kay Hunter, Cracker's mother. Although he no longer has to contend with the overwhelming problem of Billy Ray's abuse of Alma and Nicole, he will always remember the fear and terror of his ordeal in trying to resolve the problem, and he will always remember the pain and sadness he feels when he learns what Billy Ray did to Alma and Nicole and when he sees Alma in the hospital. Alma's problem of abuse has been resolved, but it has created a new problem for her—adjusting to a life without her husband's financial support and finding a means to support herself and Nicole.

Byars concludes on a positive note with Alma working in the Avondale refuge and with Cracker realizing that as long as he keeps the letter Alma has written him from Avondale "he would never lose Alma" (*Cracker*, 145). Goat calls Cracker to tell him that he is again "in deep trouble" (*Cracker*, 146), an exaggeration, of course. Byars tells her young readers that real and fictional people do not "live happily ever after."

Another aspect of the plot is the framework that Byars puts her story into. Byars's opening chapter, "An Anonymous Letter," has Cracker receiving an unsigned letter from Alma bringing fear and dread. Byars's closing chapter, "A Non-Anonymous Letter," has Cracker receiving a signed letter from Alma offering comfort and solace. Both letters are vastly different, but so are the woman who wrote them and the boy who received them.

In what would likely be a story as depressing as Bette Greene's 1973 novel about child abuse, *The Summer of My German Soldier*, Byars assuages the terror of a tale of a battered wife with laughter. Much of the humor stems from the antics of Goat and a few involving Cracker, and are often given in flashbacks. But perhaps the most hilarious incident in the novel is Goat and Cracker's "two-pillow drive" to pick up Alma and Nicole and take them to Avondale. Byars makes us feel that we are there with the boys, and laughter results despite the serious purpose of the journey and the barely escaped accidents that Goat's driving brings as he drives back on the homeward journey.

Another source of humor is Cracker's constantly running nose, which several times "runs like a faucet" and makes him long for a new type of tissue to clamp permanently on his nose, which he dubs "Pinchex."

Mr. Hunter is another source of fun. He has never been serious, and after a time his lack of seriousness and his silly comments drive Cracker's mother to divorce him: "If Jackson's mom said something like 'Don't wipe your nose on your clothes, Jackson,' his dad would say, 'That's right, Jackson, wipe it on somebody else's clothes,' and he would grab a perfect stranger's coat sleeve and say, 'Here you go, son'" (*Cracker*, 34). Reading a story to Cracker, his father changes some of the words; instead of Mother Bear's eating her porridge, Cracker's father changes "porridge" to "low-fat yogurt." He has Mama Bear complaining about someone's having slept on her "Serta Perfect-Sleeper," and the Big Bad Wolf threatening to blow down the Little Pig's "double-wide, color-coordinated mobile home" (*Cracker*, 34–35). When he calls Cracker from Los Angeles, he pretends to be the President of the United States, Queen Elizabeth, or some other famous person.

It is all these qualities of theme, characterization, plot, and humor that make *Cracker Jackson* one of Byars's most satisfying books. And all of these qualities may make it the best of the 41 books she has written to date.

Chapter Three
The Series Novels

In 1985 Byars published a chapter book, *The Golly Sisters Go West*; in 1990 and 1994 she published two companion chapter books, *Hooray for the Golly Sisters!* and *The Golly Sisters Ride Again*. With their slight plots and episodic slapstick humor that appeal to the youngest readers, these stories might be considered Byars's first attempt at writing a series if two other major series had not intervened. A year later, in 1986, Byars began publishing her first major series, the five-volume set about a most unusual southern family, the Blossoms—Pap Blossom, his daughter-in-law, Vickie; his three grandchildren, Vern, Maggie, and Junior; and his dog, Mud. Then, in 1988, Byars published *The Burning Questions of Bingo Brown*, the first book in her second major series featuring one of her most charming and delightful protagonists, Bingo Brown.

Although *The Seven Treasure Hunts*, another chapter book, features Cracker and Goat, the two main characters in *Cracker Jackson*, the two boys in *The Seven Treasure Hunts* are hardly recognizable as the same characters. The audiences for whom the two books were written are also vastly different. *Cracker Jackson* is primarily for children ages eight to twelve, while *The Seven Treasure Hunts* is designed for children ages five to seven, who are just beginning to read. Because of these disparities, these two stories can hardly be called a series.

The *Blossom* and *Bingo Brown* volumes, however, have the hallmarks of a series. Each series deals with the same set of characters, and each is set in the same time and place. Additionally, each book in each series is a self-contained story with its own theme, conflict, and resolution. The *Blossom* series often focuses on Junior, the youngest member of the Blossom family, while the *Bingo Brown* series focuses on Bingo, an 11-year-old bent on getting into what he calls "the mainstream of life."

The *Blossom* and *Bingo Brown* series do not have the same kinds of underlying seriousness of the novels discussed in Chapter 2. That is not to say, however, that both series lack serious aspects. Because the series stories have more comic incidents and situations, they seem less serious. Perhaps the major theme of the *Blossom* series is that the main characters of the story, the Blossom family and Mad Mary Cantrell, are rather antisocial and cut off from a sense of community when the series opens. By the end of the series, however, both the Blossoms and Mad Mary have been reunited socially with their community.

Adults may find the *Bingo Brown* series more amusing than youngsters, who will find the emotional highs and lows that Bingo goes through all too immediately serious and perhaps painful for them because they have similar doubts, fears, and insecurities. Simultaneously, however, they will relish the humor that comes with Bingo's relationships with his parents, his grandmother, his teacher, and his peers. These relationships will be both familiar and funny to young readers.

And though the stories in the *Bingo Brown* series are hilariously funny, they, like those of the *Blossom* series, have a serious underpinning. The transition from childhood to adolescence is a difficult time in the lives of children. In putting her protagonist through many of the ups and downs of preadolescence, Byars seeks to reassure young readers that they are not alone in experiencing the pains of growing up. At one time or another many children will find their parents embarrassing and trying, will have difficulty in dealing with the opposite sex, and will have trouble coping with a new sibling and other painful experiences like Bingo's.

The *Blossom* Series

The *Blossom* series consists of five novels: *The Not-Just-Anybody Family* (1986), *The Blossoms Meet the Vulture Lady* (1986), *The Blossoms and the Green Phantom* (1987), *A Blossom Promise* (1987), and *Wanted . . . Mud Blossom* (1991). Unlike the *Bingo Brown* series, which focuses on the main character, the *Blossom* series focus on different members of the Blossom family as well as other characters who play a part in the lives of the Blossoms; however, six-year-old Junior Blossom figures more prominently in the stories than perhaps any other character. The characterizations are rich in variety and zaniness, from Mud, Pap Blossom's dog, to Pap himself to Mad Mary Cantrell, the vulture lady, one of Byars's most appealing and unusual characters.

The *Blossom* stories place Byars firmly in the tradition of southern fiction. In the series she has four of the major characteristics common in southern fiction. First, the characters in the series are highly reminiscent of characters appearing in southern fiction since the early 1800s, including the kinds of characters that appeared in southern local-color fiction of the latter part of the nineteenth century. Second, Byars presents Mad Mary Cantrell as a grotesque character, the kind of character found in

Southern Gothic fiction since Edgar Allan Poe and continued in the twentieth century. Third, historically and fictionally, southerners have demonstrated strong affinities for family, land, and community. Fourth and most obviously, the series are set in the South, apparently in the Piedmont region of South Carolina.

It is the characters who make the series lively, refreshing, and memorable and delightful reading. The characters in the *Blossom* series are "unsophisticated, warm, ardent, impetuous." They have "an original and vigorous nature, rough, but rich, . . . [and] fresh—full of virgin glow and enthusiasm—yearning after great things and impetuous in their attainment."[1] This description appeared 150 years ago, in an 1836 issue of the *Southern Quarterly Review* describing the people of the old Southwest—the Mississippi Valley area of the South. Nonetheless, it describes the characters of the *Blossom* series as accurately as if the writer had read these stories himself.

One has to read only the first book of the series, *The Not-Just-Anybody Family*, to see how accurate the 1836 writer is in his description of these elements of the southern character exhibited throughout the *Blossom* series. The first book opens with Junior on the barn about to fly off; he stands there with his arms in wings made "of wire, old sheets, and staples—his own design,"[2] and in his "fresh" and "unsophisticated" mind, he believes he can fly. He yearns "after great things and [is] impetuous in their attainment."

Junior, however, does not reach his goal—at least, not as planned. He is about to fly when he sees a car coming down the road trailing a cloud of dust, and he soon realizes it is not Pap, his grandfather Blossom. It is too early for him to be returning from his selling the 2,147 beer and pop cans he has gone into Alderson to sell; his old rusty pickup bumper does not shine like the one on the vehicle coming down the lane to the Blossom farm. When Junior sees the blue lights, he knows it is not Pap, but the police.

Junior yells, "Police!" and goes for the door to the barn loft, but he cannot get through it because of his wings. He drops to his knees and hides under his wings. The police arrive, walk around the house, consider looking into the barn, and discover something on the roof of the barn, which begins to slide, feet first, down the steep slope of the roof. When Junior wakes up, he is in the Alderson General Hospital with two broken legs.

Vern and Maggie, Junior's older brother and sister, who have been waiting for and urging him to fly, do not want to be seen or caught by the police. They run as soon as they hear Junior cry "Police!," "one of the most dreaded words in the family vocabulary" (*Family*, 5). Equally "impetuous in attainment," they do not stop running until they have run three miles deep into the woods.

After dark when Vern and Maggie return from the woods and do not find Junior or Pap, they do find the remnants of his wings on the ground by the barn. The next day, they walk to Alderson to find Pap, now convinced that he must be in jail (after all, his pickup lacks license plates and an inspection sticker). Outside the jail at dusk, Vern gives the secret bobwhite whistle Pap has taught them, and Pap, in a third floor corner cell, answers Vern's call. With typical Blossom impetuosity and lack of sophistication, Vern decides the only thing to do is to break into the jail; he has no idea that he can walk into the jail and ask to see his grandfather. With help from a tree, a board, and Maggie, Vern goes through an outside air vent into the cell with Pap, a happy reunion. Pap tells Vern that Junior is in the hospital; he gives Vern money and Vern climbs back up to the vent and throws the money down to Maggie, telling her that Junior is in the hospital.

Just as ardent and impetuous as the other Blossoms, Maggie takes the bus to Alderson General Hospital, spending the next 12 hours with Junior, who is overjoyed to see his sister. In the bed next to Junior is Ralphie, in the hospital for the most recent of several surgeries on the remainder of his leg he cut off in an accident with a riding lawn mower. He is just as happy to see this original girl, Maggie, as Junior is, and Ralphie instantly falls in love with Maggie.

Maggie yearns "after great things," and in her unsophisticated eyes, she believes she has found them in the hospital: "she could not have been happier if she had been in the ritziest hotel in New York City. Everything she wanted, or would ever want, was right here." She eats "a pimento cheese sandwich from a vending machine, heated . . . miraculously in a small oven, and washed down with an ice-cold Mello-Yello. . . . [S]he had napped in the waiting room, on a long plastic sofa, while watching 'Let's Make a Deal.' . . . This was living" (*Family*, 104).

She casually announces to Junior and Ralphie that she is going to Pap's hearing in the courthouse. Both boys are alarmed by this news; Junior wants to attend the hearing, too, and Ralphie, not about to let his newfound love out of his sight, offers an ingenious solution to get Junior to the courthouse even though he has two broken legs and is in casts up to his hips.

Ralphie is hardly unsophisticated; in fact, Ralphie is cunningly sophisticated, but he does have the Blossom impetuosity to attain. He puts
Junior into his wheelchair, and familiar with the hospital as only a frequent patient can be, he whisks him down the elevator and out to a cab.

Maggie, Vern, and Junior, however, are not the only members of the
simple, unsophisticated Blossom family "yearning after great things and
impetuous in their attainment." Vickie Blossom, their mother and the
daughter-in-law of Pap, has already achieved considerable fame as a trick
rider in rodeos. She yearns for her and Maggie to become a pair of star
trick riders in the rodeo circuits, and she and Maggie together achieve
that goal in *A Blossom Promise*.

Even Pap's 10-year-old dog, Mud, is "unsophisticated, warm, ardent,
and impetuous." In *The Blossoms Meet the Vulture Lady* Mud's impetuosity
to attain a bit of hamburger gets him caught in Junior's wonderful coyote trap for an overnight stay in the rain before the family finds him and
lets him out.[3] His impetuosity leads him into all kinds of problems
besides the coyote trap, but his desire for attainment does not keep him
from finding a way to cross the heavily traveled U.S. Interstate 85 highway in *The Not-Just-Anybody Family*. After a long and patient wait and
then with speed, he makes it across the first two lanes of the highway
and then crawls through a drain under the second two lanes only to
come to a fence that stops him, but only briefly; Mud quickly digs his
way under the fence.

With the exception of Ralphie's sophisticated wile, all the characters
in the *Blossom* series are simple, "warm," and "ardent" folks, possessing
"an original and vigorous nature, rough, but rich, . . . fresh, full of virgin
glow and enthusiasm" (Brooks, 1090). These characteristic southern
traits help to make the *Blossom* series Byars's most southern of all the stories in her canon.

The kinds of characters Byars created in the *Blossom* series puts her in
an old and continuing tradition in southern literature. Beginning in the
Old Southwest, antebellum humorists such as Augustus Baldwin
Longstreet (1790–1870), George Washington Harris (1814–69), and
Thomas B. Thorpe (1815–78) wrote vigorous and original humor based
on the people of their adopted region. These writers often took the tall
tales and jokes and the mixture of aristocrats, back-country folks, yeo-
man farmers, local buffoons, and whoever came to hand and re-created
them in humorous and informal fiction. The tradition continued after
the Civil War, culminating in the work of Mark Twain (1835–1910),

best exemplified in *Tom Sawyer* and in *Huckleberry Finn*. Even though in the latter novel Twain takes a vigorously satirical swipe at the South and many of its traditions, Twain's characterizations and humor in both novels are a part of the tradition, which was also dominant in the work of the southern local-color writers such as Joel Chandler Harris (1848–1908) and Mary Noailles Murfree (1850–1922).

The tradition continued in this century to the present time, best represented in the humor and the sometimes outright grotesque characters in the fiction of writers like William Faulkner (1897–1962), Erskine Caldwell (b.1903), and Eudora Welty (b.1909). Of these three writers, Byars has more in common with Welty than with either Caldwell or Faulkner, though both men created humorous fiction. Welty and Byars are much alike in their creations of slightly off-center characters, such as Byars's Blossoms and Welty's Edna Earle Ponder and her uncle Daniel in the novel *The Ponder Heart* and the narrator in the short story "Why I Live at the P.O." Byars's characters, however, lack the mild spitefulness of the narrator in "Why I Live at the P.O." and the conscious and unconscious hypocrisy of Edna Earl, while Byars's characters in the *Blossom* series have the exuberance for life of both Welty's short story and novel.

This vein in southern fiction is not exclusive to adult literature or to Betsy Byars. A number of writers for children belong to the same tradition of off-center characterizations and zany humor, including Bill (1920–81) and Vera Cleaver (b. 1919), Robert Burch (b. 1925), and Robbie Branscum (b.1937).

Byars's Mad Mary in the *Blossom* series belongs to another tradition of southern fiction, the grotesque or Gothic, dating in the United States mainly from Edgar Allan Poe (1809–49) through several twentieth-century novelists of the South, particularly William Faulkner, Carson McCullers (1917–67), and Flannery O'Connor (1925–64).

Mary Cantrell, highly reminiscent of the grotesque characters of Southern Gothic fiction, is the last remnant of what was once the most prominent family in the county where the Blossoms live. In her early seventies, Mary lives alone in a remote, well-hidden cave under a high hill known as Vulture Roost, and she survives on varmint stew made from road-kill animals such as possums, squirrels, and rabbits and from wild vegetables and herbs. She dresses in long, tattered skirts and rags and men's well-worn brogans and carries a shepherd's crook. She has lived as a recluse in the cave beneath Vulture Roost for 10 years. She has no use for other humankind, has few possessions, and does not read magazines or newspapers; she does, however, have boxes of books, one of her favorites being Zane Grey's *Riders of the Purple Sage.*

Children will not recognize Mary Cantrell as belonging to the tradition of Southern Gothic fiction, though adult readers will recognize her as a grotesque. In *The Blossoms Meet the Vulture Lady* Byars portrays Mad Mary at her most frighteningly grotesque the night Junior wakes up and finds himself in Mary's cave. He has no idea where he is because Mary rescued him asleep in his own coyote trap, where he had accidentally locked himself in. She carried him, still asleep, to her cave, and when he wakes up, it is completely dark. He throws off the ragged quilts he's lying under, gets up, falls, and begins to crawl. He is relieved when he touches a shoe, then a sock, then a leg: "Suddenly a kitchen match flared above him, and Junior looked up. He saw a sight he would never forget for the rest of his life. It was a Halloween mask come to life" (*Lady*, 74–75). Out of pure fright, Junior faints. Mad Mary's appearance and outward behavior belie the softness and compassion within. Unknown to Junior when he first sees her by the light of her kitchen match, he has been rescued by Mary from his trap because she thinks someone has intentionally locked him inside the trap.

Byars's partaking of these two traditions of southern literature is not the only aspect of the *Blossom* series that puts it into the mainstream of southern realistic fiction. Southern life and fiction are characterized by love of family, love of land, and love of community. Byars reveals her kinship with early and recent writers of southern fiction through these characteristically typical elements of southern life. Perhaps the major of these elements is the love and the importance of family. Family "provides the Southerner with a sense of security, for he knows that it is made up of people like himself who understand him and his needs."[4] The Blossom family's affection and devotion are a major force in the series. Their devotion has already been seen in *The Not-Just-Anybody Family* in Vern's breaking into the jail to console Pap, and Maggie's in helping to get Junior to Pap's hearing just because he does not want to miss it. In *The Blossoms and the Green Phantom*, when Junior declares with wrenching sobs that he thinks he is a great failure, his mother, Vicki, quickly reassures him in words and hugs that he is not and tells Maggie and Vern and their friends that they are to help him in any way they can. Their devotion and affection as well as the pride they take in one another is seen in their being a "not-just-anybody family" as Maggie points out to Ralphie during her visit to

Junior in the hospital: " 'We Blossoms,' Maggie said proudly, 'have never been just anybody' " (*Family*, 99).

Southerners' love of land, another regional characteristic and often a dominant aspect of southern literature,[5] is often reflected in their keeping land inherited through several generations. Although the South is becoming rapidly industrialized and has become a Mecca for tourists and retired northerners and although most southerners do not make their living by farming, many southerners remain rural dwellers, living on small farms and in small villages and towns. Even native southerners living and working in large cities like Atlanta, Houston, and Memphis will still have close ties to their agrarian heritage, usually through relatives living in rural areas. Despite greater affluence brought to the South by industrialization, tourism, and wealthy retirees, southerners still maintain a closeness to, a bond with, the land from which their forebears wrested a living, sometimes barely sustaining. The Blossoms are rural people living close to the land. They live in the country, and the children ride a bus to school. They have a horse, and they have two dogs, Mud and Dump, that run loose. There is a great expanse of uninhabited woods and meadows adjacent to their farm, and across this uninhabited land by several miles is Vulture Roost, where Mad Mary lives in splendid isolation.

A third aspect characteristically southern and closely related to the importance of family reflected in the *Blossom* series is the significance of community, where people care about one another and their problems.[6] The importance of community forms a major theme of the series. At first, the Blossoms are self-sufficient; they rely on no one outside their family; they are so isolated from their community that the word *police* terrifies them. In Alderson, Pap drives carefully and takes side streets so that he will not become involved with the police because his license and inspection sticker have expired. This isolation from their community is also evidenced by Vern's breaking into the jail rather than asking for help by simply going into the jail and asking to see his grandfather. It is reflected in Junior's wanting to work on his inventions alone, not even wanting the members of his family to know what he is doing until he can show them the completed project.

The Blossoms' lack of communal sense begins to break down and bring them into the community with Ralphie's offer to help Junior go to Pap's hearing; it is further broken by people in Alderson helping the Blossoms—the police, reporters, and Pap's self-appointed attorney,

Henry Ward Bowman. As the news of Vern's break-in and Pap's hearing become common community knowledge, the Blossoms begin to feel a sense of security and belonging. In *The Blossoms Meet the Vulture Lady*, when the family discovers that Junior is missing late in the day after he has caught himself in his coyote trap, Pap even calls on the police to help, revealing a growing communal spirit. Because it is too dark and stormy to search for Junior that night, the police enlist the aid of other members of the community to help find Junior the next day, which the Blossoms willingly accept.

Both Maggie and Junior make friends outside the family circle, causing Vern to feel a sense of not belonging, resulting in his searching for a friend, whom he finds in Michael, a boy his age, who lives about a mile from the Blossoms. Also in *The Blossoms Meet the Vulture Lady*, the Blossoms get a telephone, that blessed and cursed symbol of communal interconnectedness: "The installation of the telephone had left Junior with the feeling that he was at last hooked up to the rest of the world, plugged in like everybody else" (*Lady*, 98).

The importance of community is best exemplified in Mad Mary, a recluse who has hardly spoken to another human being in 10 years. She has no family or friends, except Pap, and that friendship is hardly more than a tenuous acquaintance until Mary rescues Junior. Mad Mary's returning to the community is reminiscent of at least a half dozen books for young readers in which a child helps give an adult a sense of belonging to the larger human community or restores love to the heart of a cranky adult. It is Junior who starts Mary on her way back to being a member of the community.[7] After he recovers from his initial shock of seeing Mary by a lighted kitchen match, Junior—as is often the case with young children—quickly warms up to Mary and develops a genuine affection for her. More slowly, Mary develops a genuine liking for Junior as he sits in her cave or on its porchlike ledge talking and eating with her and later in their continued association. In *The Blossoms Meet the Vulture Lady* Mary's latent sense of community is already in evidence by the fact that she rescues Junior from his coyote trap, not, perhaps, so much from altruism but because she believes someone has locked him in the cage, which to her seems another "example of man's cruelty to his fellow man" (*Lady*, 49–50).

The next morning, as Junior and Mary sit on the ledge in front of her cave, Junior charms Mary with his enthusiasm and questions and compliments about her cave home and her way of life. Junior's surprise on learning that Mary reads books causes Mary's face almost to "crack into a smile" (*Lady*, 97). As they continue to visit, Mary finds that Junior is "the first human company she had enjoyed in ten years" (*Lady*, 105). A little later Mary does smile at a comment from Junior, and shortly thereafter she smiles again.

Mary and Junior become friends, and as a result Mary becomes more sociable. Pap takes Junior to visit Mary, and Mary comes to see the launching of the Green Phantom. At the end of the series the Blossoms have become well-integrated members of the community, and instead of just receiving help from the community, they are reaching out to help others. One day in *Wanted . . . Mud Blossom* Mary passes out on the roadside, and when the Blossoms discover her varmint bag and cane by the side of the road and Pap does not find her in her cave, they become alarmed and try to find her. Eventually, they learn she is in the hospital, suffering from malnutrition and worms. When she gets out of the hospital, she is released to Pap, and Mary comes to the Blossoms. Whether Mary will stay with the Blossoms or return to her cave is uncertain, but it is certain that she is well on her way to becoming again a part of the human family.

Closely related to the theme of being a part of a caring communal family is a secondary theme of loss and restoration. There are several instances in the series in which someone is lost and later found and restored. Junior gets caught in his own trap and is restored to his family. Mud gets caught in the same trap and is found by the Blossoms. Pap falls into a garbage dumpster, and though two or three people come by, no one hears or sees him until a woman whom he has frightened with his yells from inside the dumpster calls the police, who rescue him; he is restored to his family, who have been waiting all night to hear from the police, to whom they have reported his absence—something the family would not have done in the opening of the series. In a larger sense, the Blossom family in their isolation from their community are lost as is Mad Mary, but by the end of the fifth book they and Mary are no longer "lost."

Many of Byars's novels are set in the South, although generally their southern settings are not so pronounced; that is, the stories could have taken place in almost any place east of the Mississippi River or in any metropolitan area of the continental United States. Set somewhere in the Piedmont of the Blue Ridge of the southern Appalachian Mountains— most likely in the Piedmont of South Carolina—the stories in the series have some exact or similar place names from the South Carolina

Piedmont, where Ed and Betsy Byars live in Clemson. Alderson, the principal city of the series, is reminiscent of Anderson, South Carolina, near Clemson; and there is a "Stone Church Road," likely derived from Clemson's Old Stone Church Road. In the Blue Ridge Mountains, at the border of North and South Carolina, there is White Water Falls, which Byars names once or twice in the series, though more frequently she calls the falls "White Run Falls." There are one or two references to U.S. Highway 123, which runs through Clemson. Mud has to cross U.S. Interstate 85, the main north-south artery between Atlanta, Georgia, and Charlotte, North Carolina.

Using the Carolina Piedmont as the setting; exploiting the significance of family, land, and community to southerners; harking back to the early nineteenth century through contemporary humorists; and harking back to the creators of Southern Gothicism through purveyors of the genre in the twentieth century, Byars has created a set of characters reflecting the traditional mold of Southern fiction.

The *Bingo Brown* Series

The *Bingo Brown* series consists of four novels: *The Burning Questions of Bingo Brown* (1988), *Bingo Brown and the Language of Love* (1989), *Bingo Brown, Gypsy Lover* (1990), and *Bingo Brown's Guide to Romance* (1992). The series features one of Byars's most appealing and delightful characters, 11-year-old Bingo Brown, who is in the sixth grade in the first three books and in the seventh grade in the fourth one. In this series Byars has created the tour de force of a boy on the threshold of adolescence, an exposé of the sometimes stumbling and bumbling and sometimes bubbling and glowing efforts and emotions of a boy taking steps toward maturity into the turbulent "mainstream of life."

One of the main threads of the four novels deals with Bingo's relationship with girls, particularly with Melissa, one of three girls he simultaneously falls in love with in the opening chapter of *The Burning Questions of Bingo Brown*. Mr. Markham tells his sixth grade class to pretend that they are highly successful in their chosen careers, and in answer to his letter asking for advice they are to describe their careers and to give him some advice. When Mr. Markham calls on Melissa to read her letter, Melissa announces that she has two careers; she is a scientist and a rock star. The announcement "electrified Bingo. He stopped breathing." Bingo imagines Melissa taking off her white lab coat, spraying "her hair different colors" and jumping into a limousine to take her to perform in a rock concert. This mental picture makes him think of a film he has seen recently, *Dr. Jekyll and Mr. Hyde*: "He instantly fell in love with Dr. Jekyll and Ms. Hyde."[8]

Before many minutes pass, Harriet Conway says she is a conductor. Bingo is relieved because he knows he will "never lose his heart to a train conductor." But he is re-electrified on learning that she means she's the conductor of a symphony orchestra. Bingo imagines himself at a concert with Harriet directing an orchestra: "She was dressed in the outfit that the good witch wore in *The Wizard of Oz*. She even had the tiara. The wand was her baton." She points to Bingo in the front row, dedicates the concerto to him, and asks him to stand. He is so carried away with his vision that he actually stands beside his desk and bows. Mr. Markham thinks Bingo is anxious to read his letter. Sitting down, Bingo's "face burned. He was now in love with two girls" (*Questions*, 5–6).

And then when Mamie Lou tells Mr. Markham she is the President of the United States, Bingo falls in love with her as he envisions himself as "the First Gentleman of the United States of America" despite Mamie Lou's being the biggest girl in the room and his being the smallest boy. Besides, Billy Wentworth has told him she wears brassieres: "The last thing on Bingo's mind was falling in love with a girl who wears brassieres" (*Questions*, 6). But Bingo's imagined visions of himself as First Gentleman make him fall in love with Mamie Lou: "Visions mushroomed in his mind—Airforce One . . . Camp David . . . Russia. He would accompany Mamie Lou everywhere. At summit meetings he would not go shopping with the other presidents' wives. He would sit at Mamie Lou's side. They would have a ranch and he would take up horseback riding. He would be a popular First Gentleman and fill in for Mamie Lou at parades and Easter-egg rolls. Barbara Walters would—" (*Questions*, 6). Only Mr. Markham's calling on him brings Bingo back to the present.

Being in love with three girls is a serious concern for Bingo: What to do about simultaneously falling in love with three girls in the same class period? The problem of loving three girls is resolved, however, and Bingo settles on only Melissa, bringing a host of "burning" questions and an equal number of concerns for Bingo to cope with in his relationship with her. The four novels focus mainly on the relationship of Bingo and Melissa and on Bingo's relationships with other people, including his embarrassing encounters with Boots and Cici, his family, Mr. Markham, and Billy Wentworth.

Bingo and His Multifaceted Personality   It is Bingo who brings the series to life. Bingo has one foot still in childhood, one foot in adolescence, and one or two toes in adulthood. In Bingo, Byars has amassed all the joyous as well as the troubled doubts, fears, questions, concerns, confusions, and enthusiasms of an 11-year-old boy on the threshold of puberty, a young boy whose emotional structure is at best "fragile" (*Questions*, 38) and who asks, "*Is my life ever going to be calm?*" (*Questions*, 55). Bingo can be at the height of ebullience one minute and be the trough of despondency the next. His emotional ups and downs range from exuberance to seriousness, from happiness to sadness, from compassion to insensitivity, and from security to insecurity until a reader is convinced that Byars exhibits in Bingo every emotion, every question, every attitude that a young boy approaching puberty can possibly have.

It seems that through the creation of Bingo, Byars has decided once and for all to help young boys understand that their emotional swings are common experiences, as are their up and down relationships with girls, parents, grandparents, teachers, friends, bullies, siblings, and dogs. It is as if Byars knows that young boys have burning questions lacking definite answers at a time of life when boys still want and expect quick answers in black and white, clear and straightforward affirmatives and negatives. Such an assignment might sound as if Byars has written a "handbook" for boys entering puberty and adolescence—a heavy-handed book, more case study than artful fiction. The truth is, however, that the stories in the *Bingo Brown* series are about as similar to a handbook as a peacock is to a fly.

Bingo is a character of considerable complexity. Between childhood and adolescence, he sometimes exhibits the characteristics of a very young boy, but one who wants also to be in the "mainstream" of life, who wants to be mature and not have every new relationship and revelation jolt him into a disheveled emotional fervor, not to have every gnat wing throw him off the track. That Bingo still has one foot in childhood is also revealed in his sleepwear and bed sheets. He sleeps sometimes in Superman pajamas, and when he is troubled he seeks comfort in his Superman cape—"wrapped in his Superman cape, he fell asleep" (*Questions*, 46–47). Another time when he has had some bad news from Melissa about their sixth-grade teacher, he hangs up the telephone and "pulled his Superman cape around him as if he were shielding himself from the world" (*Questions*, 131). He has sheets designed for young children: Snoopy sheets, Smurf sheets, and Teenage Mutant Ninja Turtles sheets.

Perhaps one of the most obvious characteristics of young children is their self-centeredness, and Bingo can be as egocentric as any four-year-old or any 11-year old. Bingo's egocentric nature is natural and expected and adds to the complexity of Byars's portrayal. Bingo's egocentrism is reflected in several instances, but perhaps nowhere better than in his relationship with Grammy, his maternal grandmother, who indulges his every whim. When he is with his grandmother he feels he is the center of the universe: "She let him have what he wanted to eat. She let him do what he wanted to do. She loved to take him to the movies. She loved to make popcorn for him. She made pancakes in the shapes of animals. She said, 'Why, of course you do,' all the time. Like Bingo would say, 'I want ice cream on my cornflakes.' 'Why, of course you do.' *Splat*." And when Bingo's mother tells him he is to spend the weekend with Grammy, Bingo thinks, "A weekend of having every single one of his wishes—no matter how foolish—fulfilled, would do a lot for him" (*Questions*, 80–81).

In a hilariously funny scene in the second book in the series, *Bingo Brown and the Language of Love*, Bingo's being the center of his universe is knocked asunder when his father tells him that his mother is pregnant. While Bingo's reaction to the astounding news is probably fairly typical of an 11-year old learning that he or she will no longer be the only child, Bingo's reaction also reflects his egocentrism. When his father tells him the news, "Bingo let out a sharp cry of pain, an animal sound he had not known his lungs and vocal cords were capable of. He closed his eyes. He tried to regulate his breathing, to slow his racing heart, to bring his body back to the normalcy of 10 minutes ago. . . . Blindly, Bingo drew in his breath. The thought was so alien, so unthinkable that his brain refused to process it. . . . He had assumed that he would be child enough for any family."[9]

Bingo's self-centeredness is just a small part of Byars's multifaceted portrayal of an 11-year-old. It adds to the humor of the novels; it also deepens Bingo's character and adds to his appeal and charm, giving the reader a greater sense of his reality. Egocentrism is sometimes especially hard on pubescent boys and girls because they strongly feel that their every act and deed are always being seen by others, easily embarrassing them.

Bingo's vulnerability, stemming in part from his egocentrism, but also in part from his impulsive nature and his sensitivity, is common in early adolescence. His vulnerability and impulsiveness enrich his portrayal and the stories. Bingo's impulsive nature is easily seen in his falling in love with three girls almost simultaneously. His impulsiveness is sometimes accompanied and propelled by his curiosity, often resulting in discomfort. In *Bingo Brown and the Language of Love* Bingo has not a clue as to why his mother is upset, but he desperately wants to find out. After his mother suddenly leaves to go to Grammy's, Bingo looks at his mother's folded note left for his father under the VCR. Although Bingo knows the note is for his father, he impulsively reads it anyway. "The short, hurtful sentences" of the note are painful for Bingo. Again impulsively, he takes the note to the typewriter to add "Your loving wife," only to discover he has spelled "wife" as "wofe" (*Language*, 56). To Bingo, the note is so private and painful that he does not want to admit to his father that he has already read the note. These and similar episodes reveal Bingo's sensitive, caring, and considerate nature. When his dad asks him what the note says, Bingo does not want to tell him because it has hurt him, and he thinks it will hurt his father, too.

Bingo's compassion and sensitivity are a significant part of his character, and they, too, contribute to his vulnerability. In *The Burning Questions of Bingo Brown* the principal, Mr. Boehmer, announces one morning to the class that Mr. Markham has been badly hurt in a motorcycle accident. Bingo's reaction to Mr. Boehmer's news is physical; nonetheless, it shows his compassion and sensitivity. From his feet to his throat, Bingo physically reacts: "Despite the heat from the radiators, Bingo was cold. . . . Bingo's reaction was all physical. First the coldness, then the trembling, and now his throat began to tighten. He felt as if he had been the victim of an accident himself" (*Questions*, 134).

Bingo and Billy Wentworth ride their bikes out on Highway 64 to see where the accident occurred. What they see leads them to believe that Mr. Markham deliberately drove his motorcycle off the highway to try to kill himself: "The strength that had sent them speeding out . . . in a blaze of falling leaves was gone. . . . They turned their bikes around and slowly started for home." The boys' slackened strength is another example of a physical reaction, but Bingo's emotional reaction shows his sensitivity, compassion, and vulnerability heightened by a feeling of guilt. Emotionally, Bingo "felt as if eight years had passed since he heard about the accident instead of eight hours" (*Questions*, 143–44).

There is, however, another reason that Bingo thinks Mr. Markham may have attempted suicide. A few days before the accident Mr. Markham asks his students to write a letter to a friend to talk him out of committing suicide. When Bingo and Billy realize that Mr. Markham may have deliberately attempted to kill himself, Bingo feels as if he—and his classmates—were personally responsible. In explaining to his mother why he feels responsible for Mr. Markham's attempted suicide, Bingo's vulnerability and sense of guilt show. He tells his mother, "Mom, . . . maybe our letters weren't good enough. I mean, I didn't really try, because I thought it was stupid. But if I had known I was writing to him—that it was for real—if I had known that, then I really would have tried. I mean, maybe he went off the road because all of us thought the letters were stupid and didn't try" (*Questions*, 146).

Along with being compassionate and sensitive, Bingo is also volatile—a trait related to his impulsiveness. In a matter of minutes Bingo's emotions can range from high to low. In the opening of *Bingo Brown, Gypsy Lover* Bingo receives a letter from Melissa, who has moved with her family to Bixby, Oklahoma. Just receiving Melissa's letter makes him happy. Bingo "got a warm feeling just holding the envelope. If she had just sent the envelope, Bingo had thought, he would be happy." Bingo's joy in getting a letter from Melissa is short-lived, however. After the thrill he has from reading the words, "Dear Bingo," he comes to "the worst sentence he had ever read in his entire life." Melissa writes, "I finished your Christmas present today, and I KNOW you're going to love it."[10] Most people would think that a Christmas gift in the offing is a grand thing to learn, but not Bingo. Going from bliss to agony in an instant, Bingo clutches the letter to his heart, throws open his bedroom door, and stumbles into the living room exclaiming to his mother, "I just found out a terrible, terrible thing—[Melissa's] giving me something for Christmas" (*Gypsy*, 5). It's terrible because Bingo cannot think of anything that he can give Melissa in return.

And when he goes shopping for a gift, he cannot find anything that will be appropriately perfect for Melissa. He develops "shopper's block" and as a last resort goes to a bookstore ostensibly to see about a book for Melissa, but subconsciously to look for *Gypsy Lover*, a book Melissa has mentioned in her letter. At a somewhat low point emotionally, Bingo goes to the romance section to look for the book. His low emotional point is not low for long because Bingo makes a terrifying discovery: "Bingo reached out to see if there were any gypsies lurking behind the pirates and sea captains, but his hands never reached the shelf. For at that moment Bingo noticed something that put gypsies and pirates out of his mind. His arms were growing! They had grown about four inches since this morning! They were sticking out of his jacket sleeves!" (*Gypsy*,

10–11). Volatile Bingo examines himself to see if anything else is growing, which it is not, but still in a panic he does not stop to think that the cause of his alarm and concern is the sleeves of his coat, which he is outgrowing.

Bingo's volatile emotional swings are also reflected when he returns home to show his mother how fast his arms are growing. Mrs. Brown pays little attention to his panic about his rapidly growing arms and confesses that she has read part of his most recent letter from Melissa, the part where Melissa says that when she is reading from the romance *Gypsy Lover* she substitutes Bingo's name for that of Romondo, the Gypsy lover. Bingo forgets his concern about his arms. All he can do is to say "Mom!" twice "as the shock rolled over him again and again like waves." His mother apologizes, and Bingo fusses at her for reading his private mail and declares, "Mom, just because you're pregnant doesn't give you the right to do anything you want." They continue to argue about the matter—"Bingo and his mom were good arguers"—until Mrs. Brown takes Bingo's hand and lays it on her stomach so that Bingo can feel the baby move. Awed by the feel of the baby's movement, Bingo forgets all about Mrs. Brown's having read part of his letter from Melissa, and "withdrew his hand and put it in his pocket as if he were depositing something he wanted to save." When his mother asks him if he will forgive her for reading Melissa's letter if she tells him what the sex of the baby is, Bingo's surprised response is "What letter?" Bingo, who has never really liked his name, has a momentary pang of jealousy when Mrs. Brown tells him the baby is to be a boy named James Samuel. In a matter of minutes Bingo's moods go from concern, to anger, to awe to jealousy (*Gypsy*, 15–19).

Bingo's volatile nature takes him from one crisis to another; perhaps the crisis showing best his volatility comes in *Bingo Brown's Guide to Romance* when he learns from Billy Wentworth that Melissa, whom he has not heard from in three months, is in town. Because the Browns' washing machine is broken, Bingo's mother sends him—forces him, rather—to the laundromat to do the family's washing, a task Bingo does not relish. Without sorting the laundry and after stuffing it helter-skelter into the machines, he goes outside for some fresh air, glad none of his acquaintances have caught him biking to the laundry with a basket of dirty clothes. It is there that Billy finds him and tells him he has just seen "that girl." Of course, Bingo does not know which girl ("there had been many girls in Bingo's life"), but he immediately thinks of Melissa: "Bingo's heart began to thud against the Rinso box, which he had wrapped in both arms. . . . The thought of her was enough to make Bingo's imprisoned heart attempt to burst right out of his chest, through the box of Rinso, . . . Bingo said in a controlled voice, 'What girl would that be, Wentworth?' 'Melissa.' Bingo dropped the Rinso box with a thud."[11]

Bingo's volatility sometimes arises from his not knowing how to handle difficult situations. He imagines his sense of dignity will be compromised and he will be embarrassed. At the end of *Bingo Brown's Guide to Romance* Billy comes over to tell him that he has learned from Melissa's cousin, whom Melissa is visiting, that Melissa is coming to see him. At the same time, Bingo's parents decide to go out for a bit, and Bingo's mother asks him to sit with Jamie. Although Bingo protests because he does not want to be baby-sitting with Jamie when Melissa comes, he gives in when his mother says the entire family will "visit with Melissa." As it turns out, Jamie is a great help. Waiting with Jamie for Melissa to come, Bingo works himself into a near frenzy, going to the window every few minutes to see if Melissa is coming, all the while explaining to Jamie the action of a Roadrunner cartoon on television. When the doorbell rings, "Involuntarily, Bingo's arms tightened around his brother. . . . Bingo got up at once and started for the door. He held Jamie in both arms. This way he didn't have to worry about an embrace. An embrace could obviously not be accomplished without dropping or crushing or in some way endangering his brother's health. . . . He was grateful for Jamie. Anyone facing a perilous situation—and Bingo considered himself an expert on those—should hold a baby. They made wonderful shields" (*Romance*, 102–3).

Another aspect of Bingo's character is his desire to be adult, to be manly and be able to cope with all emotional jolts without their throwing him into a tizzy. His longing to be more adult is exhibited in all four novels and in various ways. Bingo's preoccupation with his mustache and shaving is an indication of his still being a child longing to get into the "mainstream of life," as he calls being manly and adult. Bingo does not realize that having a beard to shave will indicate only physical maturity, not the emotional maturity he longs for, enabling him to be calm in the face of frustrations.

In "The Groundhog Mustache," the opening chapter of *Bingo Brown and the Language of Love*, Bingo stands in front of the bathroom mirror studying his face. His mother walks by and asks if he is still admiring himself. Bingo asks her if she can see his mustache. All she sees, she says, is dirt above his upper lip. Bingo does not believe her, and as he leans toward his reflection in the mirror, he says proudly, "I would be the first student in Roosevelt Middle School to have a mustache." His father interrupts to call them to supper, and Bingo proclaims, "A lot of women would be thrilled to have a son with a mustache . . . though I'll have to shave before I go to high school. You aren't allowed to have mustaches in high school" (*Language*, 3–4). It has to be obvious to the most casual reader that it is not his mother who would be thrilled, but Bingo himself. And just as obvious is the pride he takes in seeing himself as the first student in his school to have a mustache—and a bit closer to being an adult.

Bingo thinks, or hopes, that shaving will put an end to his childhood. One afternoon while prowling through the medicine cabinet, he finds a bottle of skin bracer. Thinking he needs some bracing up, he puts a little on his face, but nothing happens: "His skin was not braced." Bingo reads the directions, something he does not usually bother to do, and he gets a shock when he reads, "apply after shaving." He thinks, "After shaving! Bingo felt these were probably the two most important words he had ever read in his life. He was so moved he had to close his eyes and hold onto the basin for support. . . . For days Bingo had felt like the helpless victim of the entire world, a toy in the turbulent mainstream of life. Now, at last, he could do something positive for himself. With one stroke of the razor, he could put childhood behind him forever" (*Lanugage*, 95). At the end of the series, Bingo is still trying to shave, and although he has taken some giant strides, he is still trying to get into the "mainstream of life." Near the end of *Bingo Brown's Guide to Romance* Bingo decides to shave before Melissa arrives. "He knew . . . a quick shave would give him the manly feeling that he needed to meet this new crisis" (*Romance*, 95).

The word "man" and related words often turn up in Bingo's thoughts and in his journal. He seems to think that using the terms will help him to become adult in feeling and action. While Cici Boles is taking his picture to send to Melissa in Bixby, Oklahoma, Bingo thinks he understands "man's weakness for having his picture made" (*Language*, 26). He does not care much for the big, blond Cici Boles and ruminates about "how just one experience with a big blonde could make a man yearn for a small brunette" (*Language*, 32). Another time, "Bingo cracked his knuckles in a manly fashion. He would have spit on his hands but they were already wet with sweat. Bingo prided himself on his manly gestures and hoped, sometime in the future, to get the mature feelings that went along with them" (*Romance*, 9). In his journal under "Goals," he writes, "Becoming a man" (*Language*, 114).

"Becoming a man" is not easy, especially when it comes to talking with girls, what Bingo refers to as "mixed-sex conversations." Bingo frequently has trouble during mixed-sex conversations because he does not know what to say or how to end a conversation, or he becomes embarrassed about something said during the conversation. One afternoon Melissa writes him a note asking him to meet her after school by the flag pole. He does not have time to talk because he has gotten into a predicament with Billy Wentworth and Harriet Conway and wants to avoid them both. Never able to end decorously a mixed-sex conversation and with dignity, Bingo is amazed that he actually ends his conversation with Melissa by the flagpole as casually as he does. When he sees angry, purple-faced Harriet coming down the steps from the school building and coming for him, he says, " 'I've got to go. I'll call you later.' As he ran down the street, he was amazed at how casual he had become, at how easily he had come up with that. *I'll call you later. Am I a man at last?"* (*Questions*, 127).

Closely related to his longing to be adult are his occasional references to getting into the "mainstream of life," a phrase he uses to signify remaining calm, rational, and capable of coping with crises without becoming upset, even to relish crises. Bingo first uses the phrase in his notebook in *Bingo Brown and the Language of Love* when he writes under one of his lists of "Trials of Today," "Continued failure in reaching the mainstream of life" (*Language*, 16). Later he uses the phrase again and extends the image when he thinks, "the entire eleven and eleven-twelfths years of his life had been one long struggle to get into the mainstream of life. Other people, he knew, were content with little pools on the sidelines, but he, he had always craved the thrill of the current. . . . Once a person gets into the mainstream of life, can he ever get out? If he does get out, can he get back in?" (*Language*, 80–81). By the end of *Bingo Brown and the Language of Love* Bingo feels that he has at least "learned to dog-paddle in the mainstream of life" (131–32).

Bingo's multifaceted personality Byars reveals through what he says and what he does, but perhaps readers learn just as much about this dynamic character through his personal relationships with others, from adults to peers to his baby brother, Jamie, born in the third novel, *Bingo Brown, Gypsy Lover*. Not only do these interactions help to reveal Bingo's character, but they also help to move the stories forward, create humor, tension and suspense, conflict and resolution.

Bingo and Girls   Bingo's relationships focus mainly on girls; but just as important, they also focus on adults—his parents, his maternal grandmother, and one of his teachers, Mr. Markham. They also focus on his classmate, neighbor, and nemesis, Billy "Rambo" Wentworth, and on Jamie before and after his birth. Bingo's relationships with others are both painful and joyful, with the exception of his relations with Cici Boles and Boots and Wentworth, which are mainly trying. And while all his interactions with others may be painful or joyful or both for Bingo, they are nearly always funny.

The adage that the course of true love does not run smoothly is accurate in Bingo's relationship with Melissa. Although Bingo and Melissa have only one major upset in *Bingo Brown's Guide to Romance*, most of their romance runs smoothly. What makes the course of Bingo's romance less than smooth usually evolves from Bingo's characteristic emotional volatility. Bingo's mother suggests more than once in the series that Bingo tends to go "totally overboard." Bingo is not a boy to miss an opportunity for a gnat's wing to throw his train off the track. When Bingo first falls in love, it is not just to fall in love, it is not even to fall in love forever, it is to fall in love "for eternity, maybe even infinity" (*Questions*, 6).

Bingo is so affected by any incident, ordinary or extraordinary, that it would be difficult for his affairs of the heart to run smoothly. One day after he has fallen in love with Melissa, he makes his roundabout way back to his desk from the pencil sharpener—a trip he makes as often as possible to satisfy his curiosity about what his classmates are doing— and pauses by Melissa's desk. He discovers that Melissa is writing to Isaac Asimov: "This moved Bingo so much that he couldn't step away from her desk. He could not move. He just stood there, staring down at her hair which was so beautiful that she didn't even need mousse. He was glued in place, rooted to the spot. He would never ever leave her desk. He would spend the rest of his life here like a pilgrim, a worshipper at a shrine, a—" (*Questions*, 33). A few days later, again on his way to the pencil sharpener, he notes with horror that Melissa is crying: "Bingo stood there, aching with sympathy, ready to cry himself" (*Questions*, 77).

In person or on the telephone, mixed-sex conversations with Melissa usually send Bingo into a tizzy. The first time Melissa telephones him, she says she has "to talk to somebody. I can't keep this to myself any longer." Bingo sinks into a chair, his heart pounding, finding Melissa's declaration to be "mysterious, intriguing," and he thinks this is "the way mixed-sex conversations were supposed to be" (*Questions*, 90). A day or so later, however, he finds a mixed-sex conversation in person with Melissa less than enjoyable because he so dreads his having to spend the night with Wentworth while his parents are out of town that he is sick; in fact, he is so sick that he has no desire to make trips to the pencil sharpener, no desire for mixed-sex conversations, and no burning questions (*Questions*, 104).

Bingo, like many pubescent boys, is so concerned about the "how to" or the "why" of something that he misses the pleasure of the moment, as he does the first time he and Melissa hold hands. How does one stop holding hands is his concern. After Mr. Markham's accident and after he regains consciousness, Miss Brownley, the substitute teacher, holds a lottery to see which two students will be first to visit Mr. Markham in the hospital. Melissa's and Bingo's names are drawn, and both are happy to have been drawn to accompany Miss Brownley. When they get to Mr. Markham's room, Melissa and Bingo hold hands; Bingo thinks "it was not romantic. Melissa was holding on too tight. It was more a mutual-strength kind of thing." They hold hands during the entire visit, and are still holding hands as they leave the hospital. As usual, Bingo is concerned, and his burning questions begin to well up: "Bingo was a little worried about the fact that he and Melissa were still holding hands. And he had no idea how to stop holding a girl's hand. Were you allowed to just let go? Would he and Melissa still be holding hands when they got to the car? How could they get in the car holding hands, with her in the front seat and him in the back? Would they have to hold hands out the window?" (*Questions*, 162–64).[12]

Any romance is difficult to keep alive when one of the pair moves several hundred miles away to Bixby, Oklahoma, as Melissa does in the second book of the series, *Bingo Brown and the Language of Love*. The day Melissa announces to Mr. Markham and her classmates that she and her family are moving to Bixby, Bingo is at the pencil sharpener. Melissa says she hopes some of her classmates will write to her. Bingo stands by the pencil sharpener and makes a vow to write every day. He will "write such letters as the post office had never seen, letters so thick postal workers would marvel at their weight. His letters would go down in postal history. Years later, an unusually thick letter would be referred to as a 'Bingo letter'" (*Language*, 12–13). Of course, Bingo does not write tomes every day, but he does at first make several long-distance calls to Melissa in Bixby. The calls suddenly stop the day his mother learns that he has been making the calls to Bixby, calls that totaled $54.29.

Before Melissa and her family leave for Oklahoma, Bingo goes over to say good-bye. Bingo's emotions continue to give him a spin, to make his affair of the heart less than smooth: "The sight of her made him weak in the knees." On Melissa's front porch, they make eye contact. Bingo feels "as if his eyes were popping out of his head." There on the front porch, Bingo discovers the "language of love." Bingo realizes that when Melissa asks, "Will you write to me?" she is really saying, "Will you love me forever?" With sudden insight, Bingo realizes, "This was the language of love" (*Language*, 65–66).

For all the dizzying highs the romance puts Bingo through, it does continue to blossom until Bingo falls out of love with Melissa. For three days, Bingo feels an emptiness he cannot explain. He eats, he drinks, but he still feels empty: "It was just a huge internal void." And then it hits him as he is walking to the grocery store with Misty, the Wentworths' dog he is keeping for them while they are vacationing. Aloud to Misty he announces the cause of the void: "I am no longer in love." Bingo decides to give himself a test to see if he has really fallen out of love. Ever since he and Melissa rode to the hospital to see Mr. Markham and she smelled of gingersnaps, he has associated the odor of ginger with Melissa, an odor that causes him to have a "burning desire" to call her. Going to the cookie section of the grocery, he picks up a pack of gingersnaps: "An expression of sorrow came over Bingo's face." He tells Misty, "it's over" (*Language*, 43–49). There is no lovers' quarrel, no angry words, none of the usual causes for falling out of love. Bingo just simply falls out of love with Melissa as easily and as rapidly as he fell in love with her.

Near the end of *Bingo Brown and the Language of Love* Bingo receives a letter from Melissa with her picture enclosed. In a parody of a sixteenth-century Renaissance love poem that explores every feature of the beloved's face, Bingo examines the hair and face of Melissa in the picture. Accompanied by flips of his stomach, he looks at her eyes, is dazzled by them and by the eye contact the picture seems to offer. He looks at her luxurious hair: "Bingo knew that from now on, every time he heard the word luxurious, he would think of Melissa's hair. When he was ninety-two, if some one said, 'Isn't the foliage luxurious this summer?' he would nod, but his brain would soar with the thought of Melissa's hair." He looks at her "jazzy" smile and her white teeth. Inspired by the picture, Bingo begins to write Melissa a letter (*Language*, 128).

The letter is well on its way to becoming one of the tomes Bingo had vowed he would write when he remembers he has looked only at the picture but has not read Melissa's letter. When Bingo reads "Dear Bingo," he goes into a tailspin. He reads "dear" with the subtleties of the language of love, and he knows Melissa really means "dearest." Bingo "had fallen out of love with Melissa, suffered, then discovered his suffering was in vain. He loved her more than ever" (*Language*, 131).

Except for the problem of what Bingo can send Melissa for Christmas, the romance is played down somewhat in the third novel of the series, *Bingo Brown, Gypsy Lover*. The romance again comes to the fore in the fourth novel, *Bingo Brown's Guide to Romance*, because Bingo has made a serious gaff in sending Melissa a photocopy of a letter he's written. Bingo learns just how rough the road of romance can really be. As usual, Bingo goes overboard. He likes his letter so much that he wants to keep a copy but inadvertently sends the photocopy. As a result, he does not hear from Melissa for three months. Later, when she returns to visit cousins in Townsville, she tells Bingo, "you don't forget Xeroxed letters. . . . They're like—so impersonal—like, I don't know—form letters" (*Romance*, 60–61).

For a time during her visit Melissa avoids Bingo and will have nothing to do with him. Having made her point about the photocopied letter and wanting to make amends before she leaves Townsville for Pickens, South Carolina, where her father has found a job, she comes to say good-bye. Jamie helps to make Bingo and Melissa's good-bye go better than Bingo expected it to with Jamie. And their conversation goes well. After Melissa leaves, Bingo says to Jamie, "you have just heard a mixed-sex conversation so great it could go down in the history of mixed-sex conversations" (*Romance*, 112).

Bingo's relations with two other girls in the stories are different from his with Melissa. Bingo likes—loves—Melissa, but what he feels for Boots and Cici is altogether different. Both girls are smitten with Bingo and make no effort to hide the fact; they are aggressive in their pursuit of Bingo and bring him considerable consternation and embarrassment. Cici Boles is a big blonde with press-on nails; she "was more like a high school girl—no, make that a college girl. This girl even had—" (*Language*, 24). What Cici has Bingo does not finish. Nor does Wentworth, who says Cici is "built like a twin-engine—" (*Language*, 36).

Melissa has written Cici asking her to take a picture of Bingo for her. Cici comes over and takes the picture, and, ostensibly to bring Misty in for Bingo, she comes into the kitchen where Bingo is cooking supper. (Bingo cooks supper to pay for the long-distance calls.) Bingo realizes that Cici is not going to leave. He ties on his apron and says, "You will have to excuse me now, I am preparing, er, chicken chests." No matter how broad the hints Bingo gives, Cici will not leave. When Bingo hears his mother coming in, he tells Cici to leave and give him the dog, but Cici has no intention of either leaving or giving up the dog. After a brief tug of war over the dog, Bingo wins, and falls back against the refrigerator: "bottles clinked. . . . Liquids sloshed. Ice cubes rattled" (*Language*, 30–33). Mrs. Brown does not quite understand what she sees and perhaps thinks the worst.

Bingo has two other major encounters with Cici Boles—"Cici, with two *i*'s, you know" (*Language*, 33), as she is wont to say when she introduces herself—and both encounters end in a manner just as painfully embarrassing for Bingo as the first. The third one, however, is definitely the last because she never plans to see either Bingo or Billy Wentworth again. As she puts it, straightforward and to the point, "I never want to see either one of you stupid nerds again!" (*Gypsy*, 111).

As in many human relationships, and particularly from his encounters with Cici, Bingo learns two lessons—lessons that indicate he is growing up, that he is at least about "to dog paddle in the mainstream of life." First, he learns that he does not always necessarily want to be liked: "He was only beginning to understand how important it was that this girl [Cici] not like him. The thought surprised him. It never even occurred to Bingo that the day would come when he would actually want to be disliked" (*Language*, 31–32). Second, he learns that when people show anger, they become caricatures of themselves. When Cici comes to Bingo to ask him to return Wentworth's gift to him she becomes angry, and Bingo notes what anger does to a person's face. Cici "turned and her face was terrible to behold. Some people should never, ever get angry, Bingo realized, because their faces aren't made for it. If they have little eyes, the eyes get littler. If they have a big nose, it gets bigger. Cici Boles was now a caricature of herself" (*Gypsy*, 111).

Boots is another girl whom Bingo wishes did not like him. The day he has shopper's block while looking for a Christmas gift for Melissa, he accidentally bumps into Boots, a new girl at Roosevelt Middle School; although Bingo does not recognize her, she recognizes him. Leaving the mall, Bingo goes to a bookstore apparently to look for a book for Melissa, but perhaps unconsciously to look for *Gypsy Lover*, the romance Melissa has been reading and mentions in a letter. Boots follows him to the bookstore, but by the time Boots arrives Bingo has already discovered his rapidly growing arms and wants to leave. Before he does he makes the mistake of telling her he is looking for *Gypsy Lover*.

A short while later Boots telephones Bingo to tell him her sister has a copy of *Gypsy Lover*; Boots volunteers to read him "the best parts," which are easy to find because her sister has read them so many times that the book naturally falls open to the good parts. To Bingo's dismay, she proceeds to read him a passage. This mixed-sex conversation makes Bingo uncomfortable. His heart begins to pound; his mother is listening; she's waiting to listen to his heart with her new stethoscope: "She grinned and turned the stethoscope toward him as if to listen in on the conversation" (*Gypsy*, 39). The conversation is difficult because Boots is rather persistent in keeping it going, but Bingo is unresponsive, causing Boots to get upset. Finally, Bingo is able to end awkwardly this uncomfortable mixed-sex conversation.

Boots calls again in a few days to apologize for getting upset with Bingo. In this series there are dozens of funny episodes, but this mixed-sex telephone conversation with Boots is among the funniest, as the conversation goes from bad to worse with aggressive and unsubtle Boots making no bones about Bingo's attraction for her. When Bingo confesses that he, too, sometimes gets upset, Boots replies, " 'I know—like in the mall that day. That's what attracted me to you.' 'What?' Bingo said. He thought he hadn't heard right. 'That's what attracted me to you!' she repeated. Bingo, learning that he had heard exactly right, let out a hoarse cry. . . . [His] heart began to sink. Although he was experienced in holding mixed-sex conversations—by this time he had had over a dozen of them—he was not experienced in ending them. And this was one of those mixed-sex conversations that needed ending."

This conversation, however, does not end, and Boots goes on to say that it was not only his being upset that attracted her to Bingo but also "that you're a writer. I love intelligence. I feel so stretched when I'm with an intelligent person." With that comment, Bingo is no longer able to speak, and what seems to Bingo an infinite silence begins. The silence lasts so long that Bingo wonders if Boots "had taken the easy way out and fainted, like girls did in olden times." Bingo then wonders why the telephone company does not have some way of dealing with great silences on the telephone. He begins to feel entombed within a wall of silence. His dad saves him, however, by reminding him that he is not to tie up the telephone, and he finally speaks and tells Boots he has to hang up. Bingo is so grateful to his dad that he tells him what he did was perfect (*Gypsy*, 68–70).

The last time Boots calls Bingo it is to explain what she meant when she asked him what attracted him to her. And then she lets the bomb fall: she will not be calling any more because her mother has forbidden her to call him. All Bingo can say is "Oh." Boots goes on to say, however, that she is allowed to take calls and that he can call her. Bingo says, "Good-bye, Boots," and hangs up: "Even an unwelcome conversation could be dealt with manfully" (*Gypsy*, 72–73). Bingo does not hear from Boots again.

Bingo and His Parents   Bingo's relations with adults are often just as filled with emotional ups and downs as his relations with girls. Bingo generally has a good rapport with his parents, but he does have his problems with them as they have theirs with him. Bingo and his parents' relationship is revealing, showing at times all three at their best and at times not. Bingo, like many contemporary children, often talks straight to his parents, telling them just what he thinks, something children of a generation or two ago would not have thought of doing.[13] For example, when Mrs. Brown confesses to Bingo that she has read part of his letter from Melissa about her substituting Bingo's name for the Gypsy lover Romondo's in *Gypsy Lover*, Bingo is angry and declares, "Ever since you got pregnant, you've been acting like you are the only person in the family who needs kindness and consideration. You do terrible things and then no one is allowed to do anything terrible back" (*Gypsy*, 17).

Just as siblings often argue, Bingo sometimes argues with his parents, especially with his mother. From her omniscient point of view, Byars twice points out that both Mrs. Brown and Bingo are "good arguers" (*Questions*, 29). In *Bingo Brown, Gypsy Lover* Bingo and his mom are arguing about her having read his letter from Melissa in which Melissa tells him she substitutes "Bingo" for "Romondo," the hero of the romance. Mrs. Brown points out that Bingo is pretty free to read others' letters— and his father's novel. Bingo says he has to read his dad's novel in case he needs his help: "Bingo felt they could keep this one going for days, weeks even. Even a year from now, if she criticized him for something, he would answer, 'Well, at least I don't go around reading people's private letters!' " (*Gypsy*, 18).

Like many parents, Bingo's parents are sometimes critical. It must be pointed out, however, that Bingo can be an exasperating if charming child. And it is only natural that both parents and Bingo will feel some exasperation toward one another. Early in the series Mrs. Brown's criticisms seem a bit hard, but as the books continue the reader comes to see that she is teasing Bingo as much as criticizing him. In *The Burning Questions of Bingo Brown* Bingo discovers styling mousse and the pleasure it brings in improving his appearance. The directions call for an "egg-size ball," but Bingo applies one "the size of a dinosaur egg." After he has applied the mousse and combed his hair, "Bingo could not move. He had transformed himself. Here, in the mirror, was not the haggard, pained face of last night. Here was the boy he had always wanted to be." Seeing how much of the mousse he has used, Mrs. Brown says, "You overdo everything" (*Questions*, 15–16).

The night Bingo chokes on his food when his mother says that the Wentworths are moving next door, she scolds him for putting too much food in his mouth at one time: "Bingo, only put into your mouth what you can chew and swallow. Don't cram your mouth with food. You overdo everything" (*Questions*, 28). Ironically, what Mrs. Brown does not know is how Bingo feels about Billy Wentworth, which caused him to choke, not that he had too much food. Mrs. Brown does not catch the cause, and like any concerned mother, she perhaps scolds in relief as much as in anger.

Bingo's mother's criticism causes Bingo at least once in the series to keep to himself his concern about a minor incident at school in which he has caused Harriet Conway to get it in for him. Harriet calls him, but he says he cannot talk because supper's ready, and he tells his mother to say he is not in if he gets more calls. Curious, she wants to know why. Bingo replies, "If I tried to tell you what had happened in my life, you would say it was my fault." Mrs. Brown denies that she would; Bingo says, "Yes, you say I create crisis, and, Mom, I don't create crisis, but I'm always standing right next to it. It's like I'm living my life in the middle of all these little tornadoes and I get swept into them and it's not my fault" (*Questions*, 129).

Mrs. Brown can be furious and funny simultaneously. She is "furious" about Bingo's long-distance calls to Melissa. Bingo wants to know if he can ask a question and wants a promise that his mother will not get mad. Mrs. Brown replies, "I'm already furious. Just being mad would be a wonderful relief" (*Language*, 8). Despite how it may sound out of context, her answer shows not just anger, but her sense of humor as well.

The two times Mrs. Brown comes home to find Cici alone with Bingo, she becomes understandably angry or annoyed, even if her anger or annoyance is misdirected because she reacts first and then finds out what is really happening. Mrs. Brown comes in just after Bingo and Cici have had a tug of war with Misty. His mother stops in the doorway of the kitchen, "taking in the domestic scene. Her eyes narrowed at the sight of the blond. . . . His mom's face tightened in a way that Bingo had never cared for" (*Language*, 33). The second time she finds Billy Wentworth, Cici, and Bingo in the Browns' living room watching Bingo's participation in the Clean Up Townsville! (CUT!) demonstration being broadcast on the evening news. Moved by a baby's putting his hand on Bingo's shoulder in one of the shots, Cici throws an arm around Bingo's neck and begins jumping up and down. Unknown to the youngsters, Bingo's mother walks in: "She spoke coolly from the doorway. 'And just what is going on here?' " (*Language*, 120).

In parent-child relationships, parents sometimes resort to a kind of force to get a child to do something he or she does not want to do. Mrs. Brown is not above using force to get Bingo to do something he had rather not do. In *Bingo Brown's Guide to Romance* the washing machine is broken, and Mrs. Brown asks Bingo to take the laundry to the laundromat, which Bingo thinks will be embarrassing and compromise him with his friends. He refuses. Mrs. Brown gives him the choice of doing the laundry or staying in his "room for the rest of your life" (*Romance*, 2). On another occasion, Mrs. Brown uses her force to bring Bingo around to her point of view. Because she and Mr. Brown are going out and do not want to take Jamie with them, she wants Bingo to baby-sit, but he does not want to. Melissa is coming over, and Bingo, already apprehensive about her visit, flatly refuses: "I can't be sitting here with a baby when Melissa comes over." When Mrs. Brown comes back with, "All right, we won't go. . . . We'll all just sit in the living room together. We'll all visit with Melissa" (*Romance*, 98–99), Bingo quickly agrees to baby-sit.

Although Mrs. Brown and Bingo have their differences and although Mrs. Brown occasionally forces Bingo to do things he does not want to, she loves Bingo and has Bingo's best interests at heart as she shows when Bingo develops a guilt complex about Mr. Markham's possibly attempting suicide. She then offers Bingo sympathy and wise counsel. Bingo pours out his worries and concerns to his mother, relating how Mr. Markham had asked the class to write letters to convince a friend not to commit suicide. Bingo thinks that the letters were not good enough, that he and his classmates did not try hard enough to talk Mr. Markham's "friend" out of trying to kill himself. Knowing the letters were not the cause, Mrs. Brown put her arms around him. "Honey, your letters didn't have anything to do with it. . . . A person is given a wonderful gift, Bingo—life. Life! And if he throws it away—as your teacher may have tried to do—if he throws it away, he's never going to get it back. Never! You can't change your mind next month and say, *Well, I'm tired of being dead. I think I'll pop back into the world.* It doesn't work that way. You slam the door shut, and you're never going to open it up again. To me, slamming that door is betrayal to everybody you slammed the door on, and it is the cruelest betrayal in the world." Bingo looked at his mother. "Oh, Mom," he said. "I wish you'd been there last week to write a letter." (*Questions*, 146–49)

Mrs. Brown often demonstrates kindness and consideration for Bingo. After Bingo becomes upset over what he thinks are his hideously fast-growing arms, Mrs. Brown pays little attention to his concern, knowing that he is simply outgrowing his coat. Later, however, she tells him to get himself a new coat. And at Christmas she suggests that he telephone Melissa, long before he's paid off his $54.29 worth of calls by cooking supper at a dollar a supper.

Just as Mrs. Brown at times shows affection and consideration for Bingo, so does Bingo show affection and consideration for her. During the seventh month of her pregnancy, Mrs. Brown begins having labor pains and goes to the hospital. Visiting her in the hospital, Bingo wants his mother to feel better, not be depressed about her fear of losing the baby; he wishes she would tease him, but she does not. She asks him what he has gotten for Melissa for Christmas: " 'Just some earrings.' Bingo wanted his mother to grin and say, 'not *gypsy* earrings?' in a taunt-ing way. He would willingly allow her to taunt him if it would help her feel more cheerful" (*Gypsy*, 61). He offers to make her some fudge, but she says she does not want fudge. Later, in one of the happiest episodes in the series soon after Jamie is born, Bingo does bring her fudge he has made: "Bingo presented the tin and his mother worked off the lid. She inhaled the aroma. . . . She looked over the pieces and selected one. She put it in her mouth and closed her eyes. Bingo stood in silence for the verdict. The fudge lasted a long time, but Bingo waited it out. 'Oh, that was wonderful,' his mother said finally. 'Absolutely wonderful' " (*Gypsy*, 114–15).

Bingo's relationship with his father is different from that with his mother. Mr. Brown is not around as often, and in general Mr. Brown and Bingo have a good relationship. The only times Mr. Brown gets upset occur when Bingo and Mrs. Brown get into one of their discussions late at night and wake Mr. Brown up. When Bingo looks to his parents for help with his Christmas present for Melissa, his father suggests he send her a rose, though he points out, "You'll have to pay to have the florist deliver it." Bingo's thoughts on his father's suggestion reveal Bingo's consideration for and adolescent tolerance of his dad. Bingo's thoughts also reveal another adolescent belief about parents—that they often lived in the Dark Ages: "Bingo didn't have the heart to tell his father a single rose might have been all right in olden days when girls pressed flowers in books and fainted at Elvis Presley concerts. Today, girls read *Gypsy Lover* and had given up fainting entirely" (*Gypsy*, 22).

In art as in life, parents help children with their crises, and sometimes children help their parents with their crises, as Bingo helps his parents when his mother becomes unhappy with his father about being too excited about her being pregnant and not sympathetic enough about her having to give up her job selling real estate. In *Bingo Brown's Guide to Romance* Bingo helps his father. Mr. Brown becomes depressed because his novel, *Bustin' Lewis*, has been rejected by a publisher. Bingo's mother worries over his depression, and so does Bingo. Bingo's mother tries to get his father out of his depressed state, but nothing works. Although she has told Bingo about the rejection, Bingo is not supposed to know about it. Finally, Bingo decides to help his father with his writing and to give him some advice—unknown to Mrs. Brown, of course. She has gone to an open house and has left explicit instructions for Bingo: "Listen for Jamie, and don't do anything to upset your father" (*Romance*, 84).

As soon as his mother has gone, however, Bingo goes to his parents' bedroom where his father is lying on the bed. He tells his father that he knows his manuscript has been rejected and that he knows how it feels because he has also had a rejection. Bingo has submitted what he calls the first chapter of a science-fiction story, two or three short paragraphs, and "asked if they wanted to see the rest of the manuscript—I didn't mention the fact that I hadn't finished writing it, of course." They continue to talk about Bingo's writing, and Mr. Brown asks him to refresh his memory about another science-fiction story set on Mau Mau. Bingo obliges by quoting the whole story: " 'Something was stirring deep within the volcano on the island of Mau Mau, and it was not lava.' His father seemed to control a smile. 'It *is* sort of short.' 'But I make every word count. If I can get a couple more paragraphs, I'll probably go ahead and put it in the mail. You need to send yours off again, Dad,' Bingo said" (*Romance*, 85–86). They continue their conversation, resulting in Mr. Brown's feeling better. Bingo has charmed and amused his father out of his depression and given him new resolve.

When Mrs. Brown returns, she finds her husband in great spirits, playing with Jamie. Bingo has saved the day, though his mother does not know he is responsible. She tells Bingo, "I don't know how it happened. I left and he was lying on the bed with his eyes closed to the world, and I come back and he's playing with Jamie. A miracle!" (*Romance*, 96).

It has to be a rare parent-child relationship in which the parents at some time do not embarrass their offspring. Bingo is no exception. His parents often cause him embarrassment. In *The Burning Questions of Bingo Brown* former cheerleaders and band members have been invited to the annual homecoming at Catawba College to participate in a special program. As former cheerleader and band member, Bingo's parents are excited about the prospect of a good time and of seeing old friends. Bingo's father leaves the room, puts on his old tight-fitting and moth-eaten cheerleading sweater and enters the kitchen doing a cheer: "Bingo tried not to appear as horrified as he was. He could not look at his mom because he felt so sorry for her being married to his dad." To his surprise, his mom applauds, gets her trumpet, and begins playing while his father does "a sort of Highland fling. All Bingo could do to help them was to pray that no one would come to the door. If anyone saw his family at that moment, the family name of Brown would go down, as they say, in infamy" (*Questions*, 35–37).

One afternoon later, his mom embarrasses him again with her trumpet practice. The incident also shows how differently youngsters and their parents sometimes see—and hear—things. Walking toward his house, he hears an "awful sound that filled the street." Rushing inside, he pleads with his mom to stop because the Wentworths next door will hear her. Then he asks her to play quietly. She says, "Fight songs are not minuets, Bingo. You're supposed to give them all you've got" (*Questions*, 96). Mrs. Brown does not seem to realize that her playing embarrasses Bingo. She thinks her playing loudly regardless of who hears it is all right; Bingo does not.

Without knowing it, parents often embarrass their children in front of their friends, as Mrs. Brown embarrasses Bingo in front of Melissa and Miss Brownley as they are leaving to see Mr. Markham in the hospital. Just as Miss Brownley starts the car, his mom tells him to behave himself: "Bingo knew his mom was going to say something like that. What did she think he was going to do—run up and down the hall, disturbing sick people? Turn over wheelchairs?" (*Questions*, 160).

In one of their infrequent "man-to-man" talks, Bingo's father embarrasses him by confessing that over the years there have been "at least ten girls that I have loved" as Bingo loves Melissa: "Bingo looked down at his hands in embarrassment. He wished his father would keep personal stuff like that personal." Then, Mr. Brown confesses that he is sometimes attracted to women he chances to meet—at Eckerd's drug store, where he fell in love with a woman spraying perfume on her wrists and in the Bi-Lo grocery store, where he fell in love with a woman who asked him to help choose a cantaloupe. Shocked, Bingo thinks, "It was bad enough to hear of old loves, old wedding ceremonies, old blue sparks. Hearing of new stuff made Bingo want to put his fingers in his ears" (*Language*, 38–40).

Although Bingo's parents, particularly his mother, come down on Bingo at times, they also realize the value of praise. After his father has embarrassed Bingo with his recitation about his being attracted to women, Mr. Brown compliments Bingo, "despite the incident of the phone bill, Bingo, your mom and I have been very pleased with you this summer." Bingo thinks to himself that "they had managed to hide their pleasure rather successfully" (*Language*, 40).

Sometimes, Bingo does not seem to understand that his mother is expressing her love for him. While she is decorating the Christmas tree, she picks up a Santa that Bingo made in nursery school, which she declares to be her "favorite ornament." Bingo either misses the point or chooses not to see it because he says, "Then you have very poor taste." She picks up a "pinecone reindeer he had made in kindergarten. The left pipe-cleaner antler was missing, and the reindeer dangled, tilting drunkenly to the right." She says it is another of her favorites; again, Bingo misses the point (*Gypsy*, 26–27).

The second time Mrs. Brown comes in to find Cici jumping up and down while hanging on to Bingo's neck, Bingo believes his mother thinks the worst, and he says, "You're thinking I invited this girl over. . . . You're thinking I called her up and said, 'Look, my mom is pregnant and has walked out on me and my dad, so this would be a good time for you to come over. We can have the house to ourselves.'" His mother replies, "You're quite wrong, you know. . . . I think you're terrific" (*Language*, 121–22).

At one time or another, many parents involuntarily cause their children to lie by pressing them too closely about something they have or have not done. It is probably a rare child who can tell the truth under the wrathful eye of a parent. Unwittingly, Mrs. Brown presses Bingo too closely, and he lies to her over a matter of little consequence to anyone except her. Because a boy at Roosevelt Middle School wore a T-shirt with "something vulgar on it," Mr. Boehmer decrees that no student can wear a shirt with any words. The students are unhappy, and when Bingo tells his mother about it, she declares it unfair to punish the whole school because one boy wore a vulgar T-shirt. She jokingly suggests that Bingo lead the students in staging a "wear-in" to protest, but Bingo does not know she's joking and takes her seriously. Bingo knows he is not capable of leading a wear-in, so he writes a note to Billy Wentworth telling him his mother has suggested a wear-in protest. Wentworth becomes the leader of the wear-in. Bingo is pleased that the wear-in will become a reality and pleased to be able to tell his mother about her role in it. But she is not at all pleased with his incriminating her. To calm her anger, Bingo resorts to lying, telling her that he really did not "say you person-ally suggested it" (*Questions*, 58–59).

As far as Bingo is concerned, however, his planning to participate in the wear-in shows that his parents take pride in him even if they have some mild misgivings about his taking part. At supper the night before the wear-in is to take place, Bingo announces that Mr. Boehmer will stand at the front door and send home every child with writing on his or her shirt: "Needless to say, I and every other red-blooded student in Roosevelt Middle School will have on such shirts and will be sent home." Bingo puts "food in his mouth. While he chewed, his parents had time to register doubts about the wisdom of a rebellion. . . . But they couldn't help themselves. They were too proud. Bingo could see their pride in the way they inflated themselves with air. They didn't inflate like that very often" (*Questions*, 64).

As Bingo says, his parents do not often "inflate with pride," and sometimes they seem to laugh at him, but once, when they can and have reason to, they do not. Melissa's hand-made gift to Bingo is a puzzle to him and his parents. None of them can figure out what it is. Finally, Bingo discovers Melissa's instructions and her picture of him with the notebook holder she has sent him. The situation is charmingly humor-ous, and the contrast between Melissa's picture of Bingo with his suit on and his notebook holder in his hand and the picture he sees of himself in the mirror is delightful and funny: "In Melissa's diagram, he wore a dig-nified suit and appeared to be holding a businessman's briefcase. In the mirror beyond, he saw a more realistic picture. There, he wore short, wrinkled pajamas and appeared to be holding a ladies' purse. His parents regarded him without expression. They sometimes did this just before they exploded into laughter, which, to be honest, Bingo felt they now had every right to do." His parents wish him good night, and he wishes them one in turn. He waits to see if they will explode in laughter when they return to their room, but they do not: "Sometimes, to Bingo's surprise, he found he actually loved his parents" (*Gypsy*, 46–47).

Bingo's relationship with his parents is more typical than atypical. Throughout the four stories, Bingo and his parents grow and develop, and their parent-son relationship improves. Byars has made sure that their relationships are consistent, believable, realistic, and psychologically sound in motivation and in cause and effect. True to life, it is trouble that helps them to grow and brings them closer together.

Trouble begins when Mrs. Brown learns she is pregnant. It is upsetting because she has just gotten her real-estate license and her first decent job and because Mr. Brown evidences too much happiness about another child. Mr. Brown's lack of sympathy or understanding about her possibly having to give up her new job and his overly enthusiastic response to the news of her pregnancy send Mrs. Brown home to her mother, leaving Bingo and his father alone for several days and nights. The separation bothers Bingo, and he tries unsuccessfully to help bring his mother back home.

The family grows and develops not only from the separation and its causes and outcome, but also because Mrs. Brown has a problem with the pregnancy and because of their concern over Jamie's being born prematurely. It is not just trouble, however, that brings the family closer; it is also the daily proximity, the daily give-and-take of living together, that enhances their relationships.

Aside from his relationships with his parents, another major familial relationship in Bingo's life is with his baby brother, Jamie. Byars handles this relationship adroitly, realistically, and delightfully—and satisfyingly for readers. When Bingo first learns he is to be a brother, he is understandably upset. Bingo, however, comes to accept his mother's pregnancy and to look forward to having a sibling. With consummate skill, Byars traces Bingo's acceptance of his mother's pregnancy from the initial news to Bingo's total acceptance of and affection for Jamie.

At times, when a mother first becomes pregnant, many children of Bingo's age have difficulty in talking with their mothers about their pregnancy. Bingo is no different. The first time he talks with his mother after he learns she is pregnant, he feels awkward, made more so because his father is listening to Bingo's side of the telephone call: " 'Dad told me about your, er, problem. Maybe problem's not the right word. Maybe I should have said your difficulty, your'—he swallowed manfully—'pregnancy' " (*Language*, 85).

Bingo, His Brother, and His Grandmother   That Bingo's mother goes to stay with Grammy, her mother, does not help in his adjustment to his becoming a brother. Her leaving only adds to his difficulty. When he joins his grandmother at a Clean Up Townsville! protest, Bingo complains to his grandmother, "When this baby is my age, I'll be twenty-four." His grandmother replies, "So what? I'll be seventy-four" (Language, 106).

The first realization of what a sibling might mean to Bingo comes a few minutes later at the protest. Among the protesters is a young woman with a baby. Standing by Bingo, the woman holds her baby, who pats Bingo on the shoulder. Bingo "hadn't known babies brought comfort! He only thought they had to be comforted, changed, pacified. This was a whole new concept" (*Language*, 108). The morning Jamie is born, Bingo recalls how he reacted when he learned about the baby; he confesses to his grandmother, "All I thought about was how a baby would upset my life, *my* life. . . . And now I realize that, well, it would have upset my life, but there's such a thing as a welcome upset . . . a very pleasant upset" (*Gypsy*, 97).

While he comes to realize what a sibling may mean to him, Bingo also has a pang of jealousy about the baby to come. His jealousy results from his mother's telling him that the baby will be named James Samuel Brown and will be called Jamie: "Bingo had a moment of such terrible jealousy that he would not have been surprised to look into a mirror and discover he had turned green." Bingo is jealous because his brother will have a real name, not one like "Bingo," a nickname given to him by his mother because the doctor had capriciously cried "Bingo" the moment he was born. Feeling jealous and sorry for himself, Bingo thinks his mother "would probably then continue and do all the wonderful, loving things that she had not done with him. He would be the imperfect, clumsy older brother, with gorilla arms" (*Gypsy*, 18–19). Later, however, when he asks a nurse who helped the doctor deliver him if the physician said "Bingo" every time a baby was born and learns that he did not, Bingo feels "better about his name and himself" (*Gypsy*, 75).

Bingo may have momentary pangs of jealousy, but on seeing the small, new babies in the hospital nursery when he goes to visit his mother before Jamie is born, he loses all feelings of jealousy. Bingo likes going by the nursery where the nurses put the newborns into red Christmas stockings before they go home: "Bingo enjoyed seeing the little round faces peering seriously, yet hopefully, out of the red flannel stockings. Babies made extremely nice stocking stuffers" (*Gypsy*, 75).

After Jamie is born, however, Bingo loses his heart to his somewhat premature and tiny new brother. Of course, the fact that he and his parents and grandmother go through a tension-filled period before Jamie is born makes him want a baby brother all the more. When he and his grandmother get off the elevator on the fifth floor of the hospital to visit Jamie the first time, Bingo, who has had an urge all morning to see Jamie, breaks into a run down the corridor: "He was like Roadrunner, with his legs moving so swiftly they were an invisible blur to all the considerate people who were stepping aside to let him pass." At the nursery window, he sees Jamie. He "would have known him anywhere." After he and his grandmother stand at the window for a while, admiring Jamie and talking about how he looks and his grandmother explaining why he has a tube in his umbilical cord, she says she wants to visit Jamie's mother. She asks if he wants to come, too: " 'In a minute.' . . . She left and Bingo drew closer to the window. He wanted to welcome his brother in private" (*Gypsy*, 102–5).

Later, when Bingo calls Melissa and tells her about Jamie, she says he will "make a wonderful big brother." Bingo says, "I'm going to try. . . . It's something I really want to succeed at" (*Gypsy*, 118). And he does try. The title of the fourth book in the series is also the title of the book Bingo has been writing, "*Guide to Romance, A Record of the Personal Ups and Downs of Bingo Brown. Dedicated to My Brother, Jamie, as a Guide and Comfort to Him When He Finds Himself, as He Surely Will, upon the Roller Coaster of Life.*" Bingo intends it to be a book for Jamie that will contain, among other things, accounts of "romantic problems with their solutions" (*Romance*, 3).

Another familial relationship important to Bingo is with his grandmother—Grammy, as he calls his maternal grandmother. Although Grammy seems to be somewhat idealized, she is a far cry from the stereotypical grandmother of fiction and popular imagination. She is not plump, white-haired, apron-fronted, fond-of-all-children, cookie-making, and cookie-jar-keeping. She is not a grandmother sitting at home in her rocking chair knitting and watching daily soaps. As readers see her mostly through Bingo's eyes and feelings, it is reasonable for Byars to portray her as slightly idealized. And as far as Bingo is concerned, his grandmother is perfect: "Bingo loved his grandmother. . . .

Bingo's grandmother was perfect. She did not have one fault. She let him have what he wanted to eat. She let him do what he wanted to do. She loved to take him to the movies. She loved to make popcorn for him. She made pancakes in the shapes of animals. . . . Also his grandmother called him by his real name—Harrison—which was very refreshing after all the Bingos" (*Questions*, 80–81).

Grammy is not a stay-at-home grandmother; she is an activist, "a charter member of CUT!—Clean Up Townsville! And . . . she was leading a protest at the convenience store where *Penthouse* and *Playboy* were being sold" (*Language*, 53). The motto of her life is, "Unless we leave the world better than we found it, there is no justification for our existence" (*Language*, 104).

The only time Bingo doubts that Grammy might be less than the perfect grandmother occurs when Mrs. Brown has left Bingo and his dad and is staying with her. He asks Grammy to "let her know that I forgive her" for leaving him and his dad: " 'Harrison . . .' Her voice was low, as if she were chiding him, but since she had never chided him before in his entire life, that could not be possible" (*Language*, 106).

When Mrs. Brown, already in the hospital, has to be rushed to the delivery room, Bingo's dad wakes him up and drops him off at Grammy's. As Grammy and Bingo wait through the rest of the night to hear from Mr. Brown, the relationship between Bingo and Grammy is highlighted. She has just given Bingo his first ever cup of coffee, albeit, Sanka. Bingo does not like the taste: "What he liked was the feeling of companionship that came over two adults when they sat drinking a basically bad-tasting liquid together" (*Gypsy*, 89).

In the companionable warmth of their late-night talk Bingo tells Grammy about what a good day he has had—one that he calls "practically the highlight of December," except for his concern about his unborn brother, afraid he will be born too small. Grammy assures Bingo by saying that the baby will weigh four and half pounds. Bingo demands to know if she has ever seen four-and-a-half pounds of hamburger—certainly not an apt description for the moment, but the gaff Grammy does not notice or chooses not to notice; she kindly tells Bingo that four and half pounds "might not have been enough in the old days, but today they have special care for premature infants. They can work miracles" (*Gypsy,* 90–91).

Grammy suggests again that Bingo lie down on the sofa, but Bingo says he does not want to miss anything: " 'What could you miss? Sitting at the table with an old woman!' 'Where's the old woman?' Bingo asked gallantly. This was a standing joke between them. 'I don't see any old woman.' This caused them both to smile and Bingo said, 'All right, I'll lie down if you promise, *promise* you'll wake me when the phone rings'" (*Gypsy*, 94–95).

Bingo's grandmother has another quality that Byars does not name but that she builds into the character of Grammy through what Grammy says and how she says it. Through Grammy's actions and speech, Byars shows her to be kind, patient, thoughtful, considerate, and loving—qualities best evoked through character and action. From the preceding quotations, it is obvious that Grammy possesses these qualities, further evinced in her concern over how Bingo may react when he sees his premature brother for the first time. As they drive in silence toward the hospital, Grammy begins to talk, kindly preparing Bingo for what might be a disappointment when he first sees Jamie because he is premature and will be likely have a bad color, be puffy, not a perfect-looking baby. Bingo assures Grammy that he knows what newborn babies look like and adds, "I never saw one that was really and truly what you would call ugly" (*Gypsy*, 102).

Bingo, Mr. Markham, and Wentworth   Outside of his family, another adult relationship important to Bingo is with his sixth-grade teacher, Mr. Markham. A rather unorthodox teacher, Mr. Markham rides a motorcycle and sometimes wears a "Beethoven or Bust" T-shirt. Collectively, he usually refers to his students as "gang" instead of the more customary "class" or "students." He uses an unorthodox method to quiet his students. When the students become noisy, he closes his eyes. That means "he did not want to hear one single sound." Once, when the students forget the rule, he says, "Make as much noise as you want to." They make only "a moderate amount of noise. 'Is that the best you can do? You disappoint me.' They . . . [make] a lot of noise with whistles and catcalls. Mr. Markham . . . closed his eyes. There was silence" (*Questions*, 21).

Although Mr. Markham is unorthodox, his students seem to like and respect him. Bingo was happy to have gotten Mr. Markham as his teacher, but he sometimes has doubts about why he was happy to have been placed in his class (*Questions*, 4). And when Bingo's mother questions Bingo about Mr. Markham's stability—she has heard that he had his former class write to a woman to persuade her to go out with him—Bingo defends Mr. Markham: "Well, we've never done that. . . . Anyway, he does stuff like that to make life interesting. What do you want him to assign—*My Summer Vacation*?" (*Questions*, 65). Mr. Markham's teaching

methods are sometimes unorthodox, particularly his writing assign-
ments. Once he asks his students to write a letter to his girlfriend,
Dawn, to talk her out of breaking up with him. But his most unusual
one is his asking them to write a letter to persuade a friend not to commit suicide. As the story unfolds it become increasingly obvious that
something is bothering Mr. Markham. It is not until Billy Wentworth
and Bingo ride their bikes out on Highway 64 to see where Mr.
Markham's accident took place that Bingo is convinced that Mr.
Markham attempted to kill himself and that it was not an accident.
Bingo feels that he and his classmates are largely responsible for not
helping Mr. Markham more than they did when they wrote letters talking a friend out of committing suicide. As pleasant as Bingo's relationship generally is with Mr. Markham, his apparent attempt at suicide is
Bingo's most traumatic experience in the series. Learning to cope with
such difficult experiences is a part of growing up, a part of learning to
accept responsibility for our actions and to give up guilty feelings when
we are not responsible for others' behavior and actions.

There is perhaps hardly an adult alive who cannot remember a bully
from his childhood, and if there was not a bully then there was at least
some person who was so intimidating that he or she became a kind of
nemesis. Bingo's bully and nemesis is Billy "Rambo" Wentworth, who
sits directly in front of Bingo in the classroom and whose family moves
next door to the Browns in the first book of the series, giving
Wentworth instant access to Bingo via Bingo's bedroom window. Bingo
never refers to his nemesis as Billy, but always as Wentworth.
Wentworth always calls Bingo "Worm Brain," an ironic appellation
because Bingo is obviously mentally superior to Wentworth, though not
physically superior; in fact, Bingo is physically afraid of Wentworth.

With the compassion of a mosquito, Wentworth is a foil for Bingo; he
is the exact opposite of Bingo—tough, crude, insensitive, and possessed
of a bravado that would make his hero, Rambo, blush. He is the only
boy Bingo knows who does not use deodorant and who sweats "like a
man" (*Language*, 118). The only time that Wentworth shows that he is
less than the Rock of Gibraltar occurs when he and Bingo go out to
check on the place where Mr. Markham had his accident. When Billy
sees blood on the ground where Mr. Markham landed, he turns pale and
has to lean against the trees for support and falls to his knee as he
returns to the road. He even asks Bingo not to tell about his weakness:
"Don't tell anybody, but I can't stand the sight of blood." And for once,
he does not call Bingo "Worm Brain" (*Questions*, 142–43).

Bingo's feelings about Wentworth are nowhere better seen than the evening his mother announces that Billy Wentworth is moving next door. Bingo and his parents are eating supper, and Bingo is mentally going over some of the burning questions of the day, fiddling with his food: "He kept sitting there, sifting through the questions, discarding some, keeping others, and at the same time he was making shish kebab on his fork—one lima bean, one piece of macaroni, one square of ham. Bingo liked to mix his flavors." Bingo is paying little attention to the "chatter of his parents," and when his mother announces that the Wentworths are moving next door, the announcement sends Bingo and his carefully constructed shish kebab into a choking tailspin: "As soon as the name *Wentworth* was spoken, the two lima beans, two pieces of macaroni, two squares of ham all went directly into Bingo's windpipe" (*Questions*, 26–27).

For all his dislike of Wentworth, however, Bingo does admire him at times, perhaps envies him. Compared with Wentworth, Bingo is a shrinking violet as reflected in Wentworth's accepting the challenge Bingo throws at him to lead the T-shirt wear-in, not that Wentworth needs the challenge. All he needs is to have the idea put into his head. On the playground during recess after he has gotten Bingo's note suggesting the wear-in, Wentworth climbs up on a garbage can, getting everyone's attention and says, " 'I got an announcement. . . . Let me put that another way. I got a command. . . .' Wentworth's face was so stern, so hard, he made Rambo look like a wimp." Wentworth commands everybody to wear a T-shirt with something written on it for Friday's wear-in. At that moment, Bingo admires Wentworth. Bingo is so impressed with Wentworth's daring and manner that he "put his hand on his throat to keep his heart from going up any higher" (*Questions*, 53–54).

It is mainly through Bingo's interpersonal relationships with family, girls, Mr. Markham, and Wentworth that Byars plots the *Bingo Brown* series and reveals the character of Bingo and furnishes the series with humor, suspense, and conflict and resolution, helping to make the series an outstanding revelation of the psychological and emotional pains of a boy. Bingo is every boy who has ever had questions about himself and his relations with others, a boy who will help other young readers, male and female, to understand and know themselves and others better. Furthermore, it is Bingo's relationships with others that produce the significant and important underlying themes that add immensely to the quality of the series, including a boy's first tentative steps in dealing with girls and the attendant emotional concerns of those steps; his dealings with guilt over an attempted suicide that he feels he might have kept from occurring; his coming to accept, to love, and to appreciate a young sibling; and his learning that parents are human. Perhaps the most significant underlying theme of the series is that although conflicts exist in our relations with others, conflicts are a part of life, that "wonderful gift" that Mr. Markham almost throws away. And learning to accept and understand that conflicts are a natural part of life will keep us from "slamming the door" on the wonderful gift of life. Indeed, the *Bingo Brown* stories are a celebration of that wonderful gift—a gift that comes with ups and downs, trials and triumphs, and sorrow and happiness.

Chapter Four
Style, Satire, and Irony

Three major elements of Byars's fiction are her style and her use of satire and irony—elements that any writer can use in fiction for children. Every writer for children has a style, and Byars is no exception; she has a style that is hers and hers alone. Some writers of children's fiction may use satire in some form or another just as other writers may use irony. At times, Byars uses both satire and irony to heighten or make more graphic an idea or theme she wants to stress.

The elements of Byars's writing that make her style uniquely her own are her manner of weaving disjunctive topics and character into a finished story, a kind of tapestry. Byars's style reflects her personality, education, knowledge, and background. Her style is also seen in her unique use of language to create various cadences and rhythms; vivid, graphic pictures with words connoting motion, color, and kineticism; and moods and emotions. Byars makes extensive use of figurative language, especially similes and metaphors, that young readers readily understand and that are appropriate to her plots, themes, and characters. She also uses figurative language to help create and delineate character.

Few writers of children's fiction use satire and irony as Byars does in many of her stories. Satire may be somewhat rare in children's fiction. When writers for children use satire for humor, however, they are likely to have an underlying purpose to heighten awareness of the absurdities of some human actions and institutions to correct them. Though Byars's satire is primarily for humor, she has another reason for using satire—to show that emphases on physical beauty are often misplaced and to reveal the artificiality and superficiality of some beauty pageants and some of the contestants, as she does in *The Summer of the Swans* and in *McMummy*. Byars often uses characters' names to satirize the thoughtlessness of those parents who give their children bizarre names, as she does in several of her novels, including *McMummy, The Two-Thousand-Pound Goldfish*, and *Good-bye, Chicken Little*. In *The Pinballs* Byars satirizes shallow romantic series novels, and in *The TV Kid* she satirizes mindless addiction to witless television shows as well as the false appeal of cuteness.

Byars often makes use of irony in her stories, but perhaps the best example in her canon is the ironic juxtapositioning of appearance and reality as a major theme in *The Glory Girl*. Using the ironic discrepancy between appearance and reality as the primary undergirding of an entire novel about pseudo-religiosity is unique in children's fiction.

Style   Betsy Byars's style is obviously narrative-based, but usually narrative with a twist. She frequently tells a story not with a straight time line but episodically, with flashbacks and anecdotes of the past and near present woven over her basic narrative framework. It is not uncommon for Byars to begin a story in medias res going forward for a bit and then coming back to a time before or concurrent with the section begun in medias res. In other words, Byars rarely writes a story with a straightforward narrative line. For example, in *The Pinballs* she takes a diverse group of characters—three abused children with diverse personalities and problems, a mean parent or two, a set of elderly twins, and a pair of kind foster parents and weaves them on the warp of a time line and a plot that brings the three children together in the home of foster parents, who help the children overcome, at least partially, the abuse—intentional or unintentional—they have suffered. The story begins more or less in medias res with a number of flashbacks. Like any good artist with a loom, Byars takes a myriad of diverse elements and weaves them into a patterned whole, a work of art.

If my friend, Mark Steadman, who teaches creative writing, assigned his students to write a unified, chronologically ordered chapter for a book with two parents and their 11-year old son, a latent mustache, a telephone bill for $54.29, a stir-fried supper, and a confession, all tied together with ginger and undergirded by humor, he would likely be met with dismay, shock, and groans. His students, however, would think about the assignment and try to write it, but the results would probably range from bad to good, but not very good.

In "The Groundhog Mustache," the first chapter of *Bingo Brown and the Language of Love*, Byars gives herself this same assignment. She takes these diverse elements and writes them into a unified, chronological whole. She begins with "Every time Bingo Brown smelled gingersnaps, he wanted to call Melissa [his girlfriend] long distance." Standing before the bathroom mirror admiring his latent mustache, he gets a whiff of ginger, but he does not know where it's coming from. His mother walks by the bathroom and asks if he's still admiring himself, and he asks her to verify the fact that he has the beginning of a mustache on his upper lip, which she denies, seeing only dirt.

Bingo's father tells them that supper is ready, and as she goes into the living room, Mrs. Brown picks up the telephone bill. She explains she's having trouble with the telephone company over a bill for seven long-distance calls to Bixby, Oklahoma. Mrs. Brown points out to her husband and son that she has told the telephone company that the Browns do not know a soul in the whole state of Oklahoma, "much less Bixby." Bingo manages to confess that he made seven calls to Melissa in Bixby. In a brief flashback, Bingo reminds his mother of earlier asking her if he could call Melissa and showing her the postcard he had received from Melissa with "Greetings from Bixby, OK" on it. The upshot of the discussion is that Bingo is not to touch the telephone.

Finally, Bingo helps himself to the stir-fry and realizes that the odor of ginger is coming from it, driving him mad. If the smell drives him mad, "what would the taste do to him? Would he run helplessly to the telephone? Would he dial? Would he cry hoarsely to Melissa of his passion while his parents looked on in disgust . . . ? The taste of ginger fortunately did not live up to its smell" (*Language*, 8–9). In the next to the last sentence in the chapter, in his notebook, Bingo again refers to ginger, giving a framework of ginger to the chapter.

There is more to style than pulling diverse elements together into a unified whole. Style reflects the writer's personality. A major aspect of Byars's personality is her sense of humor, and it is reflected in this chapter and in dozens of others throughout her canon. Byars's education, knowledge, and background are also reflected in this chapter. Her education is reflected in her ability to choose appropriate language and to write complete sentences and paragraphs into a unified whole. Her knowledge of children and parents is obvious, drawn from her reading and her observations of parents and children, including her own.

Throughout the *Bingo Brown* series Byars's subject is an 11-year-old boy on the threshold of adolescence; Byars clearly knows her subject, reflecting her knowledge and her background, including her study of psychology and human nature. The purpose of the series is to amuse and to entertain while showing children, particularly boys, that their emotional ups and downs at this stage in their lives are little different from what others their age experience.

In the above quotation from "The Groundhog Mustache" Byars reveals other elements of her style; she uses a mainly iambic rhythm, and she uses the four questions, one after the other, to indicate the mental maelstrom Bingo is going through. The language of Bingo's thoughts is typical of Bingo—simple, direct, with few frills except for "passion," just the kind of intense and dramatic word Bingo frequently uses, and just one of the ways Byars uses language to reveal what a character is like. Of the 33 words in the four questions, all but *Melissa, telephone,* and *disgust* are derived from Anglo-Saxon or Middle English, and 25 are monosyllabic. The first three short sentences, followed by the two-part longer fourth question, all made up of mostly monosyllabic words, Byars uses to convey the intense turbulence of Bingo's emotions and nervousness.

In *The Midnight Fox* Byars has several passages describing the black vixen of the story. These descriptive passages show her skill in creating with words motion, color, and kineticism, attesting to her stylistic talents and confirming the adage that a picture is worth 1,000 words. The vixen's

> steps as she crossed the field were lighter and quicker than a cat's. As she came closer I could see that her black fur was tipped with white. It was as if it were midnight and the moon were shining on her fur, frosting it. The wind parted her fur as it changed directions. . . .
>
> The fox crouched low. She did not move. I could see her head above the grass, the sharp pointed ears. She waited, and then slowly, without seeming to move at all, she stretched up, rising tall in the grass. She paused.
>
> Her eyes watched the grass. Suddenly she saw what she was looking for, and she pounced. It was a light, graceful movement, but there was power in her slim black legs, and when she brought her head up, she had a mouse between her jaws. (*Fox,* 42, 64)

These passages are filled with strong, active verbs and verbals of motion. The combination of short and longer complex sentences help to convey the stillness and the quick and undulating movements of the fox. In the first paragraph the leitmotif is color and movement; in the second and third paragraphs it is a taut stillness and quick motion. The last two paragraphs have a dynamic, climactic arrangement that begins tensely with two short sentences, followed by two longer, more complex sentences, and the short "She paused." In the fourth sentence, the short and long vowel sounds and the soft sibilants of the rest of the second and third paragraphs convey the fluid grace and agility of the vixen's movement.

At times, Byars's skill with words results in a sentence so powerful that it expresses the feelings of a character and reader, and like candle light reflected in a mirror, it doubles the intensity of feeling. An example of this kind of sentence occurs in *Cracker Jackson*. Taken out of context, the diction and the potency of the sentence may not be fully realized, but within the context, it is fraught with terror. After Cracker's mother learns from him about how much danger his beloved Alma is in from her husband, she makes an appointment with Alma to come to the Hunter apartment at three o'clock. She tells Cracker to go to his friend's house because she does not want him at home when Alma comes. Unknown to his mother, Cracker does not go to Goat's house but waits for Alma outside behind the mailbox. When she does not show up at three, Cracker continues to wait. At 10 minutes of four, his mother's Cutlass hurtles from the garage; although Cracker tries to get her attention, she drives quickly and recklessly away, neither seeing nor hearing Cracker. Cracker grabs his bicycle and races to Alma's house. When he gets there the house looks empty and deserted. The doors of the house and garage are shut: "The only thing to indicate either place was occupied was a line of baby clothes in the sideyard, the terry-cloth jump-suits and the tiny jeans limp in the still afternoon air" (*Cracker*, 115). It is the last climactic words of the sentence, "limp in the still afternoon air," particularly *limp* and *still*, that connote and indicate the tragedy and confirm Cracker's worst terror of what has occurred inside the house a few minutes earlier. Both Alma and her baby are lying in the hospital, "limp in the still afternoon air."

Byars's writing is filled with frequent similes, less frequent metaphors, and an occasional extended simile, graphically related to incident, character, or place. In *The Cartoonist* Byars has a paean to a junkyard that had once belonged to the father of the protagonist, Alfie, when Alfie was about five years old. The paean to the junkyard contains three similes and a metaphor that convey what it meant to Alfie and why he thinks of it still as having been a place to escape to. The

junkyard covered seven acres. On top of the concrete building where his father conducted business was a huge crown made of hubcaps.

To Alfie, the junkyard had been as good as Disneyland. Car after car, some brand new, some rusted and old, an ocean of cars that would never move again. To crawl into those cars, to work controls, to sit and dream was as good as a ride on a roller coaster.

Alfie especially like to sit in the old Dodge sedan because every window in it was cracked and splintered, so that when the sun shone through, it was as beautiful as being in church. And the Chrysler

Imperial—its windows had a smoky distortion, so that, beyond, figures
seemed to float through the junkyard like spirits through the cemetery.[1]

This paean contains several aspects showing Byars's skill with frequent similes and her less-frequent use of metaphors. The first of the
similes, "as good as Disneyland," evokes the variety the junkyard offers,
and the second, "as beautiful as being in church," evokes a quiet, spiritual beauty. Both similes are within the easy grasp of young readers. The
third one, "like spirits through a cemetery," as musical as it sounds, is
perhaps not as easy for children unless they have seen the animated car-
toons featuring Casper the Ghost or have some knowledge about
specters. Even so, the simile still works because of the sibilants in *spirits*
and *cemetery* and the preceding *smoky distortion* and *float*, which explain
the simile itself. The metaphor, "an ocean of cars" is graphic, making the
size of the junkyard more understandable than the concept of its seven-
acre size.

But there is more to the passage than its similes and metaphors;
Byars uses sound and rhythm and varied phrase and sentence lengths.
Part of the beauty of the paean comes from Byars's juxtaposing sibilants
with the hard "c" and "k" sounds throughout the passage. Just before
the analogy of old cars as akin to a roller-coaster ride, Byars has a series
of lilting, up-and-down phrases echoed by the repeated infinitives
adding to the rhythm and music of the paean. The active verbs and verbals—*covered, move, to crawl, to work, to sit,* and *to dream*—connote slow
movement like a roller coaster going up to a peak before a rapid down-
ward glide.

In her use of figurative language, Byars does not write down to children, but she often uses images that her young readers will readily
understand and identify with. In *The Midnight Fox* Byars has Tom
express his fascination with the black fox by comparing his interest in
the fox with his obsession with a new game—an obsession many children have experienced. Tom says that his fascination "was like when
Petie Burkis first learned to play Monopoly, and that was all he wanted
to do—just play Monopoly" (*Fox*, 65). In *The Pinballs* Harvey tells Carlie
each person is due 15 minutes of fame during a lifetime. Carlie says she
is going to use her 15 minutes by going on television in a shiny, low-cut
dress and make hers last by stretching "it out like an all-day sucker"
(*Pinballs*, 5). Show me a kid who does not know what an all-day sucker
is, and I'll show you a kid who has been reared by 80-year-old twins who
do not believe in candy. In another simile, Byars uses common, ordinary

salt and pepper shakers, one with slightly larger holes than the other, to show that the Benson twins are "exactly alike except that one's eyes, nose and mouth were a little bigger than the other's. They looked like matching salt-and-pepper shakers" (*Pinballs*, 5).

In an extended simile in *The Summer of the Swans*, Sara Godfrey uses an erratic ride on a seesaw, another object well-known to children, to explain what her life has been like during the summer the story takes place. The passage also shows Byars's skill in capturing the cadence and language of a girl's speech. Sara tells her retarded brother, Charlie, "I'll tell you what this awful summer's been like. You remember when that finky Jim Wilson got you on the seesaw, remember that? And he kept you up in the air for a real long time and then he'd drop you down real sudden, and you couldn't get off and you thought you never would? Up and down, up and down for the rest of your life? Well, that's what this summer's been like for me" (*Swans*, 16).

In *After the Goat Man*, which deals with change and upheaval in the lives of Ira Gryshevich and his grandson, Figgy, and Figgy's newfound friend, Harold V. Coleman, much of the imagery is related to nature and animals, highly appropriate for a story set in the hills of West Virginia and about people living close to the land. Lying on his back, overweight Harold "felt like a beached turtle" (*Goat*, 16); another time, because he is slow, he feels "like a box turtle" (*Goat*, 51). "Figgy's mind often worked on instinct, like an animal's. He could sense approaching storms and other natural disasters" (*Goat*, 81–82). Figgy thinks of people being connected, "all wound together as if they were caught in one huge spider web" (*Goat*, 56). When Harold arrives at the area around Mr. Gryshevich's cabin, where the highway department has bulldozed all the trees, it looks "as if a tornado or freak wind had come ripping through the forest and up the valley, a wind strong enough to sweep the land clean, to part the forest" (*Goat*, 103).

Byars uses similes to delineate character. A number of images in *After the Goat Man*, also drawn from nature, reflect the character of Ira Gryshevich. Rising from the sofa, he "would uncoil like a snake" (*Goat*, 23). Figgy thinks of his grandfather as strong, capable, and unwavering "like nature, like a stream" (*Goat*, 94). Harold sees Mr. Gryshevich's physical shape as "big and solid, bent forward like an old tree" and his face as "craggy, tough . . . like granite" (*Goat*, 106).

Byars uses metaphors less frequently than similes, but she uses them in the same ways. In *The House of Wings* she uses a metaphor to help establish the setting of the story. Sammy's first encounter with his grandfather's dirty, run-down house and messy, cluttered yard causes him to think, "This was a wilderness" (*Wings*, 21). A quick movement of Sammy's grandfather makes Sammy see "a young man in an old disguise" (*Wings*, 65). In a graphic and effective metaphor, Byars describes Sammy's splashing water during Sammy's initial attempt to swim as "a blaze of water" (*Wings*, 141). Her use of *blaze* suggests frenzied, vigorous movement as well as color, height, sound, and heat; using a term associated with fire in connection with water gives the metaphor an unexpected or paradoxical quality; the term is no less effective, however, because shapes of splashes of water resemble flames.

Satire   Satire in children's fiction is unexpected; nonetheless, it is there. It rarely occurs in picture-book realism or fantasy, though there are some exceptions such as James Marshall's *Yummers!* (1972), a delightfully humorous satire on the obvious cause of obesity (and by extension a satire on overindulgence of any sort). Mild, humorous, but a little more obvious and biting, satire sometimes occurs in fiction for children eight to twelve years old, and becomes progressively less mild, but rarely pungent or bitter, in literature for adolescents.

Satire pokes fun at human follies, foibles, and institutions with the purpose of reforming by making us laugh at our erratic, eccentric, and idiosyncratic beliefs and behaviors. In fiction for children, satire is usually gentle and funny and is perhaps used mostly for humor, but who can say for sure whether the writer had humor or reform or both in mind? Byars's novels are among the funniest for young readers, and one of her ways of creating humor is through satire.

As a nation, we like spectator sports and beauty pageants—among a few things that we tend to go overboard on. No town or city is too small or too large for a beauty queen. There's a beauty pageant for just about every crop grown in the United States, giving rise to reigning queens from Miss Alfalfa to Miss Zucchini; there's a beauty pageant for just about every human activity and endeavor; somewhere, there must be a pageant for Miss Sorghum Molasses and a pageant for Miss Save the Purple PolkaDotted Newt.

Byars does not mind getting in a lick about beauty pageants. In *The Summer of the Swans* Sara Godfrey hears some boys yell, "Hey beautiful!" Sara turns around and too late painfully realizes the cry is not for her, but for Rosy Camdon, "who was Miss Battelle District Fair and Miss Buckwheat Queen and a hundred other things" (*Swans*, 91). To have a girl serve as Miss Battelle District Fair or Miss Buckwheat is a mild "put down," a gentle satirical thrust at empty-headed girls and parents who think that winning the title "Miss Pumpkintown" or "Miss Pancake Queen" is a worthy achievement.

In one sense, a central theme of *The Summer of the Swans* has a satirical twist. Byars may be indirectly satirizing some adolescent girls' beliefs that beauty is the most important thing in the world and that hardly noticeable features girls exaggerate into gross and glaring abnormalities. Being a woman and having three daughters in their adolescence about the time she wrote *The Summer of the Swans*, Byars was surely familiar with the adolescent dissatisfaction that Sara feels about herself.

The stereotypical brainless beauty queen Byars satirizes more pene- tratingly in *McMummy*. Valvoline Edwards is a frequent entrant in local beauty pageants, and while Mrs. Mozer fits her dress for the next pageant, Valvoline rehearses her "philosophy" of life that she will give before the pageant judges and audience. The dearth of sincerity, origi- nality, and the triteness of her philosophy reflect her superficiality, not to mention her lack of grammatical acumen with "only" modifying "pass" instead of "once": "My philosophy of life is this. Be not what your are, but what you are capable of being. Make very minute count. Spend time with yourself and your other loved ones. You will only pass this way wunst."[2] Mrs. Mozer has to correct her pronunciation of "once." If she wins the contest, Valvoline has her winner's speech ready, which is just as vacuous as her philosophy: "I owe my success to God and to my country and to my boyfriend Bucky Buckaloo" (*Mummy*, 15). Valvoline is also limited in talents; "other contestants can sing and toe dance—one of them is a real ventriloquist—and all I do is twirl a baton—and half the time I drop that" (*Mummy*, 74). When Valvoline drives Mozie, Mrs. Mozer's son, to Professor Orloff's greenhouse, she has to have Mozie point out the controls for headlights and windshield wipers and tells him she would "turn down the air-conditioning if I knew where it was" (*Mummy*, 26–27).

Byars is not above poking a little satirical fun at parents who give their children bizarre names, such as Valvoline's mother has given her. Valvoline's mother thought she was naming her for a character in a romantic novel, but got the name mixed up with a brand of motor oil. Valvoline's name is not the only name in the Byars canon that suggests Byars may be giving a dig at parents for their thoughtlessness in naming children. In *The Pinballs* the 88-year-old Benson twins are named

Thomas and Jefferson because their father admired President Thomas Jefferson. The three sisters in *The Two-Thousand-Pound Goldfish* are named for spices—Pepper, Saffron, and Ginger. Nearly as good are the rhyming given names of Mrs. Little and her two sisters in *Good-bye, Chicken Little*: Laurena, Helena, and Karena.

In *The Pinballs* Byars satirizes shallow romantic series novels, popular with adolescents and adults alike. Byars, through Carlie, pokes fun at their superficial formulaic plots and characterizations. Carlie has already read three in a series featuring nurse Laurie Myers: *Hong Kong Nurse, Peace Corps Nurse,* and *Nurse of the Yukon,* only the first she liked. The other two she did not like, "Not enough romance" (*Pinballs,* 41). At the library with Harvey she discovers *Appalachian Nurse,* one in the series she has not read. It takes Carlie only a few seconds to read the novel; she reads two or three sentences at the start, another a little later on, and five at the end. As she and Harvey leave the library, she declares to Harvey, "You know, it was almost as good as *Hong Kong Nurse*" (*Pinballs,* 69–70).

Elizabeth Segel suggests that in *The Cartoonist* Byars satirizes the misuse of television (Segal, 59). In *The TV Kid* Byars satirizes our—children's and adults'—addiction to witless and pointless television. Lennie, the protagonist, is so caught up with the giveaway quiz shows that he cannot study; the satire is also pointed at the quick and easy solutions, the false resolutions, the facile endings of many television dramas that give an untrue picture of what life is really like.

In *The TV Kid* Byars may be holding up for ridicule our penchant for letting the cute, camp, and false betray us in her portrayal of the Fairy Land Motel that Lennie's mother has inherited. With its concrete figures from folk tales and Mother Goose and its imitation wishing well decorating the grounds, the Fairy Land Motel is a monument to kitsch and bad taste. Lennie's grandfather may have used the figures and the wishing well with its blue fake water painted in the bottom as a kind of drawing card for travelers, a means of getting the attention of customers. There is a falseness and artificiality about the concrete wishing well and the figurines just as there is something false and artificial about the television programs that Lennie is addicted to. The name of the motel, the well, and the concrete figures are a gimmick to draw in customers, just as some television programs use gimmicks to hook viewers. The name, the well, and the concrete figures do not tell guests whether the beds are comfortable and the rooms are clean.

Byars is using the addictive television programs and the tackiness of the Fairy Land Motel for more than satire. The programs Lennie is addicted to and the picture she paints of the motel and its grounds give immediate insight into the characters. Edna Earle Ponder, the loquacious monologist of Eudora Welty's *The Ponder Heart* says, "Show me a man who wears a diamond ring, and I'll show you a wife beater."[3] By the same token, good or bad, what our tastes are tells something about us.

And by satirizing brainless beauty pageant contestants, the somewhat bizarre names parents sometimes give their children, shallow romantic novels, mindlessly addictive and falsely resolved television programs, and our taste for camp and tackiness, Byars makes us aware of and able to laugh at our foibles and idiosyncrasies. At the same time, she creates humor and delineates character.

Irony   There are many forms of irony, but irony usually means a writer is saying one thing while meaning something else. Irony of situation occurs when the opposite happens of what we expect. Byars has both kinds in her canon, but she has more situational irony. In *The Dancing Camel* Abul, the buyer of Camilla, the dancing camel, buys Camilla so that he can exploit her dancing, but ironically she does not dance in the marketplace as Abul had expected her to. In *The 18th Emergency* it is ironic that Marv Hammerman comes up just as Mouse Fawley is writing Marv's name under the picture of Neanderthal man on the hall chart depicting the history of early human beings. Mouse has no idea that Marv, the school bully with the muscles to go with his bullying, is anywhere near him.

Irony may also mean that a writer can present an anecdote, episode, or an entire work in an ironical vein as Jonathan Swift does in "A Modest Proposal." That is, a statement, an anecdote, an episode, or an entire work may have two or more completely unexpected or incongruous, hence ironical, meanings. Byars uses this kind of irony in *The Glory Girl*. The basic incongruity or irony of *The Glory Girl* is the differences in appearance and reality. There are two basic kinds of characters in the story—those who appear to be good, pious, kind, and loving but are not, and one or two who appear not to be good and kind but are.

The family of John and Maudine Glory make their living by going from place to place in an old, ramshackle blue school bus singing hymns and selling tapes of their singing. John Glory is the father of the Glory children, who make up the "Glory Gospel Singers" except for Anna, who cannot sing, and Maudine, John's wife, who accompanies the singers on the piano.

"John" is a biblical name, most often associated with the apostle John, the writer of the Gospel of John and the book of Revelation. John is often referred to as the apostle of love because of the kind and loving disposition he displays in his gospel. John Glory, however, hardly lives up to his namesake's disposition. Unctuously and with false enthusiasm, he serves as master of ceremonies when the group sings publicly. A vain man, he dyes his hair and has it set in a permanent wave; he wears a scarf to hide his sagging neck. He smokes one Pall Mall cigarette after another, except when the singers are performing. He is cowardly and emotionally weak, covering both cowardice and weakness with a self-righteous anger and bravado. Stubborn to the point of stupidity, he is hypocritical, giving off an unctuous air during performances that puts him in the company of Dickens's Uriah Heap. In other words, John Glory is not the man he appears to be.

John Glory does not like Newt, his ex-convict brother, perhaps because he was always jealous of him, as Mrs. Glory reveals to Anna, because Newt was Grandma Glory's favorite when they were children growing up. Unintentionally, Mrs. Glory also reveals that even early in his life, John Glory had a self-righteous, hypocritical stance. Readers also need to remember that the source of this information is John, not Newt. Mrs. Glory tells Anna, "This thing between [Newt and John] goes way back. When they were little boys, their mother liked Newt best. No matter what John did—and he was the one who made the good grades and did the chores and went to church. He had medals every single year for perfect church attendance. When he went to 4H camp he even got notes from the counselors that he'd attended services so he could keep his record. But no matter what he did to make them proud, Newt was always Grandma Glory's favorite."[4]

Maudine Glory, hardly the picture of a good mother or a loving human being, plays the piano for the family's practices and concerts. Byars says, "She had been playing the piano since she was four years old. She never had to look at the keys" (*Glory*, 31). Maudine is partial to her daughter Angel though she denies it when Joshua, one of the twins, accuses her of liking Angel the best. Not a good liar, her neck and face redden as she denies Joshua's accusation. Later when the family is in the hospital after their bus accident, Maudine spends more of her time with Angel than with any of the other three children.

Like John, Maudine is vain. She proudly wears her hair in a seven-inch-high beehive: "She automatically puffed her beehive hairdo. . . . She was only four feet eight inches tall, and she was proud of her hairdo, which made her five feet three" (*Glory*, 8). Maudine is on the hefty side and has small feet and hands. Unable to discipline the twins, Joshua and Matthew, and perhaps finding her daughter Anna uninteresting, she is indeed partial to Angel, the prettier of the two girls.

"Maudine" is a name parents sometimes give to children because they like the feminine ending and the combined sounds of the diphthong and vowel; the feminine ending makes the name sound more delicate than "Maud" by itself. "Maudine" is reminiscent of "maudlin," derived from "Maudelene," or Madeleine (Mary) Magdalen, who was often depicted by Italian painters with eyes swollen from weeping.[5] To associate Maudine Glory through her name with the saintly Mary Magdalene is ironic, because Maudine is not saintly.

Angel Glory is pretty, a good singer, and about as scintillating as a 10-penny nail. She is a foil for Anna. Like her parents, Angel is vain and self-absorbed. She rolls up her hair every time the family returns from a concert, no matter how late it is; she rolls it up again the next day, whether it is warranted or not. Her selfishness is obvious when the family stops to eat a late-night supper at a pizza parlor. She and Anna order a pizza together; Angel eats only the pepperoni slices, which she picks off delicately with her fingers, leaving Anna only the sauce and crust.

There is irony in her name. Angel is not angelic although she can sing angelically—at least, "Audiences always got quieter when Angel sang" (*Glory*, 114). She has a doll-like face; her blank preoccupation with her hair, "thick, golden, Rapunzel-like" (*Glory*, 11), which she loves, causes her to wonder how "people who didn't have nice hair amused themselves" (*Glory*, 12). Her name and hair bring to mind the artificial angel hair people sometimes use for decorating Christmas trees. Associating Angel's hair with angel hair hints at the artificiality and lack of substance of Angel herself.

Obviously, Joshua and Matthew have biblical names. Joshua was a man of God, who, after the death of Moses, led the Israelites. Matthew was a tax collector who became an apostle and a biographer of Jesus. Ironically, neither Joshua nor Matthew has any of the qualities of these two men of God. Joshua and Matthew constantly misbehave, argue, fight, and cause trouble. They are uncontrollable, always in motion and full of meanness—two more characters in the ironic menagerie Byars has created in *The Glory Girl*.

Anna Glory does not fit the Glory mold; she cannot sing, and she is so deprived of a sense of rhythm that she cannot even play the drums. During a concert she sits quietly at the back of an auditorium, waiting till a concert is over to open her cash box and sell tapes and albums of the family's recorded songs. Anna is shy and retiring, a kind of nonentity, just a good girl with none of the falseness of the other Glory family members. There is little, if anything, ironic in Byars's portrayal of Anna. The irony lies in the fact that Anna is not like the other members of her family, as might be expected.

Newt Glory, however, appears to be a bad man. Newt has just been paroled from prison, after serving seven years for robbing a bank. Early on, he accidentally burns his parents' house down and then runs away. In the navy he gets off his battleship in Manila and then misses it because he cannot find his way back to it. After he is paroled, the Glorys meet his bus, but he is not on it. Newt is extremely shy, and it seems surprising that he has robbed a bank. He and a companion pull the robbery with their faces covered by ski masks; but in an ironic twist, because his companion has severely bowed legs, the police are able to identify him and Newt. Ironically, readers know as much about Newt as any of the other Glorys even though he appears only rarely. At first, readers may get a prejudicial view of the kind of person Newt really is because we learn about him from Mr. and Mrs. Glory.

Newt's shyness and timidity Byars emphasizes in his reluctance to contact the Glorys after he is released from prison and in his demeanor. Although she does not know it is Newt, the first time Anna sees him, he comes in out of the rain near the end of a concert and stands at the back of the auditorium in the shadows, his head down, his hat "in his hands in an old-timey gesture of politeness" (*Glory*, 58–59). He offers to buy a tape, but Anna, sensing the man has no way to play it, refuses to sell him one. He steps back, pulling into his wet overcoat, reminding Anna of a turtle. Newt's name is the same as that of the newt of the salamander family—shy, retiring amphibious animals living in or near ponds and streams or on damp ground beneath stones and logs or in cool, dark, and damp crevices or caves. Byars heightens the association of newts and Newt in that he seldom appears in the story except when it is dark and raining.

Newt, like his brother, John, is not what he appears to be. He has the reputation or appearance of a bad man; in his sister-in-law's eyes he is inconsiderate. His timid, retiring behavior and much else about him seem to indicate that he is neither courageous nor self-sacrificing. Yet he is by far better than his brother. He never speaks harshly and is always kind to Anna, the only member of the family he speaks to. Most of all, however, and despite his timidity and seeming lack of courage and honor, he puts his life on the line to save the Glory family from drowning the night their bus plunges off the highway into a flooded creek. With Anna's help, he saves his sister-in-law, who has held a grudge against him for years; he saves the children, hair-rolling pretty Angel, the rotten twins; and he saves his brother, John. Newt appears to be a man with a bad reputation—a bank robber and a convict—but in reality he is good, brave, and honorable.

As it deals with the differences in appearance and reality, the incongruity of what most of the Glorys appear to be and what they really are, *The Glory Girl* is probably Byars's most ironic story. There is another irony or paradox related to *The Glory Girl*; it is Byars's only book dealing with religion, or to be more exact, with a pseudo-religious family. Byars is a southerner, and her stories, since she moved from West Virginia to South Carolina, have been set in the South, sometimes referred to as the "Bible Belt"—a belt that is, some say, still rather firmly buckled. What may also be unexpectedly ironic is that with the exception of *The Glory Girl*, religion plays only a small part in her stories set in the South.

All good writers have a unique personal style, but few use satire and irony as consummately and effectively as Byars does in many of her stories. Her satire usually has a twofold purpose: to create humor and to make a serious point. Irony involving the discrepancy between what a character expects and what actually occurs is fairly common in children's fiction. Byars makes use of this kind of irony in several of her novels besides *The Dancing Camel* and *The 18th Emergency*. This kind of ironic undergirding to emphasize the differences in appearance and reality that Byars presents in *The Glory Girl* is rare in children's fiction.

Chapter Five
Elderly Characters

Perhaps no other contemporary writer for children has the number of elderly characters that Byars has in her canon. From *Trouble River*, published in 1969, through *Coast to Coast*, published in 1992, Byars has created at least 12 elderly characters ranging from the somewhat idealized grandmother in the *Bingo Brown* series to the miserable and disgruntled Pap, Alfie's grandfather, in *The Cartoonist*. Other contemporary writers of realistic fiction for children have created elderly people, but not as many as Byars has, and few with the freshness, vigor, reality, and diversity of Byars's characters. A number of writers have created one or two memorable and finely drawn elderly characters, including Onion John in Joseph Krumgold's *Onion John* (1959), Mr. Hilton in Robert Burch's *Two That Were Tough* (1976), the twins' grandmother in Katherine Paterson's *Jacob Have I Loved* (1980), and Jimmy Jo's grandmother in her *Come Sing, Jimmy Jo* (1985). Equally memorable are Theodore Taylor's Timothy in *The Cay* (1969) and Sharon Bell Mathis's 100-year-old Great-Great Aunt Dew in *The Hundred Penny Box* (1975).

Like Charles Dickens's Aunt Betsy Trotwood in *David Copperfield* (1849–50) and his Miss Havisham in *Great Expectations* (1860–61), Byars's elderly characters tend to be eccentric in one or more ways; and as Dickens frequently does, Byars "tags" her elderly characters with a recurring motif or favorite word or phrase. Alfie's grandfather, Pap, in *The Cartoonist* is disagreeable, constantly harping against the government, often asking who will pay for the government's foolish mistakes. When he tells Alfie that the president of the United States has given the Russians 20 million bushels of grain, Pap asks his tag question of who will pay for it and gives his tag answer, "You and me." Pap tells Alfie that the Highway Department is $6 million in debt and asks his usual question and gives his customary answer, "Yeah, you and me who don't even own a car" (*Cartoonist*, 7–8).

Among Byars's eccentric elderly characters are the 88-year-old Benson twins, Thomas and Jefferson, in *The Pinballs*. These two sisters are remarkable, not only because they are twins, but also for Byars's quick, deft portrayal. Byars devotes little time to the twins, but the few details she gives makes them loom large in readers' eyes as full-blown and eccentric characters: "They were the oldest living twins in the state. Every year on their birthday they got letters of congratulation from the governor" (*Pinballs*, 5). Named for their father's favorite president, the twin sisters' peculiarities are many, including their first names, Thomas and Jefferson, and their saving as a memento the tree limb that killed their 96-year-old father. Their saving the limb is a telling example of their and other older people's idiosyncrasies. That is not to say that younger people might not save the limb that gave the death blow to a parent, but they are not as likely to: "The father would have lived longer except that a limb fell of a tree and hit him on the head. The twins had kept the limb on the back porch for a long while, and the only time the twins had ever been angry at Thomas J was when he, not knowing the importance of the limb, had broken it up for firewood" (*Pinballs*, 15).

When the two sisters lie dying in the hospital, Thomas J and his foster parent, Mr. Mason, visit them. Byars creates a sadly comic dialogue between Thomas J and Jefferson that captures the language and concerns typical of the elderly and their worries about valuable or cherished possessions. The incident also indicates something about the character of the old ladies and the paucity of their lives. They seem to realize they are dying, and their instructions to Thomas J are like a last will and testament as one or the other reminds him not to let things go down, to can the peas, and to get their father's gold watch and their three gold coins.

Just as eccentric as the Benson twins is Uncle C.C. Cushman in *Good-bye, Chicken Little*. Uncle C.C. is 92 years old, though he claims to be 100. He "had learned there were more advantages to being a hundred than any other age. When the Baptist ladies came visiting, they made a special fuss over him because he was a hundred. On Sundays he sometimes stood at the front door and told every visitor, 'I am one hundred.' Sometimes he thought to add, 'today,' and was showered with congratulations and candy bars. He intended to be a hundred years for the rest of his life."[1]

Uncle C.C. is childishly self-centered and somewhat senile, his senility demonstrated in his forgetting what happened recently, though he seems to have total recall of the past, especially if he can make himself the hero of whatever tale he's telling. When he tells Cassie about the Spanish-American War, which he was not in, he puts himself into his brother's role, who was in that war. Later he tells a story about his winning a spelling bee in which he had not even participated. He takes the role of

Wilma Darrell, who won the bee by spelling down his sister with "receipt."

Uncle C.C.'s childishness is reflected in his temper tantrums. While visiting the Littles, he tells Jimmie about a time he verbally attacked a woman in the nursing home because she complained, "Life has no meaning." He becomes so upset recalling the incident that "he could see the woman clearly in his mind. . . . She had cringed back from his fury, genuinely afraid. She had held up her thin arms for protection. This had only made him madder. He had wished for his grandfather's cane with its huge silver knob so he could bop her over the head. 'You want meaning,' he had screeched, 'look at a giraffe' " (*Chicken*, 71–72).

On his way to spend Christmas with the Littles, Uncle C.C. becomes angry with Mrs. Little, his niece, because she has come for him and not his nephew Pete, who has drowned. He asks why Pete did not come for him, and, frustrated because her car has stalled and will not start, she snaps at him, "*Be quiet!*" He searches for an insult and remembers an old woman at the nursing home who yelled "Ungrateful trash!" at everyone. He turns toward Mrs. Little and yells, "Ungrateful trash!" (*Chicken*, 48).

Uncle C.C. is cantankerous, suspicious, and confused, as shown in his believing that Mrs. Little is secretly planning not to take him to the nursing home where, he is sure, he is missing something important. A nervous Nellie driver, Mrs. Little has a reasonable excuse—a heavy downpour—for not going when Uncle C.C. wants to. Cassie's boyfriend offers to drive Uncle C.C. back, and still thinking Mrs. Little is trying to trick him, he fights her off with an umbrella when she comes to escort him to the car: "He struggled with Mrs. Little, feebly pushing away her arms. The woman was an octopus, he thought. He batted at her many arms as if they were flies" (*Chicken*, 99).

Sammy's grandfather in *The House of Wings* is another major elderly character, a credible picture of independent old age. He is no stereotype of the kind and loving grandfathers of much children's fiction. The old man is a red-letter character, ranking with Mad Mary in the *Blossom* series. The first time Sammy sees his grandfather is at night when he and his parents drive up to his grandfather's house in Ohio. To Sammy, his grandfather gives "the impression of a wild old man" (*Wings*, 15). The next morning, Sammy thinks, "His grandfather looked wild even in the daylight. He wore an old railroad man's jacket and a cowboy's shirt and miner's boots. Sammy didn't think his grandfather had been any of those things. . . . The miner's boots were too narrow, and he had cut out the sides. . . . His army pants were big and loose because he had sewn some extra cloth in each side. . . . His skin had the soft dustiness of leather" (*Wings*, 22).

As remarkable as the old man's appearance is, his personality is what sets him apart. He recognizes "the preciousness of life," reflected in the care he devotes to his birds and in the kind of attention he gives Sammy as well as in his rescuing the blind and wounded crane. His love of birds is evident almost from the outset of the story. When Sammy first goes into his grandfather's house, he finds a goose sleeping in the hallway. Over the years Sammy's grandfather has had a number of birds, and he still has an owl, a parrot, and several geese, all of which have the run of his house. He tells Sammy he has "had birds living with me the best part of my life" (*Wings*, 54). His obsessive passion is birds; he tells Sammy stories about some of the birds he has had in the past; as much as anything, it is his grandfather's love for birds that finally attracts Sammy to him.

Sammy's grandfather is not materialistic. He has let his house and yard run down since his wife died 10 years earlier; his dress and total disregard for his appearance indicate the same. He has no use for being stylish, keeping up what others might consider a respectable appearance.

Like Mad Mary in the *Blossom* series, Sammy's grandfather is a recluse. He does not seem to have much contact with others and little desire to do so. There is no mention of friends or neighbors, only birds. A revealing and sad commentary on the old man's personality is that he does not keep up with his own children, who seem to mean no more to him than his run-down house. He tells Sammy that he has never been able to keep his daughters straight and says, "I got a son living in Louisiana that I wouldn't know if he jumped out from behind that bush yonder. . . . But, boy, I'll tell you something. I could pick my owl and blackbird and my gray parrot and my canary and my wild ducks out of a thousand" (*Wings*, 74).

The first elderly character in the Byars canon is Grandma in *Trouble River*, a historical novel set in the nineteenth century. Dewey's parents are away, and Grandma is sleeping in the cabin when Dewey comes up from the river to discover an Indian from a small marauding band about to enter the cabin. Deciding that safety lies down the river, Dewey, his grandmother, and the dog Charlie take off on Dewey's homemade raft, the "Rosey B.," only eight by six feet, unwieldly and difficult to maneuver. Though essentially a flat, static character, Grandma is more memorable than not. Cranky, querulous, and feeble, Grandma walks with a cane, and even with it she nearly always has to have help from Dewey. Byars's descriptive verbs and adverbs in introducing Grandma's dialogue help to reveal her character. She speaks "testily," "stubbornly," "irritably," and "distastefully," and she "grumbles" at Dewey.

Grandma is critical. When she and Dewey start down the river, Grandma complains about the river and Dewey's raft: "I don't trust this here river. Ain't neither one of them anything to look at."[2] Even the first time she saw the raft, the raft "stunned" her because she was expecting something on the order of the steamboats and keelboats she had seen on the Missouri River. Grandma frets and fusses her way down Trouble River, as much a burden for Dewey as the clumsy raft and fickle current. Grandma may be a kind and sweet old lady, but if she is, it does not show. Safe at the end, Grandma walks towards Hunter City still grumbling.

That Byars portrays Grandma as a rather cranky old woman in one of her early realistic stories shows that although Byars was still something of a novice in creating realistic fiction, she was a keen observer of people and able to incorporate her observations into realistic (if somewhat one-dimensional), credible, and consistent characters. Grandma may be cranky and difficult, but she is never mean or mean-spirited. The grandmother—Grandma—in *The Two-Thousand-Pound Goldfish* may not be mean either, but if she is not mean, she comes closer than any other elderly character in the Byars canon.

In fiction and in television advertisements, grandmothers tend to be stereotypes—kind, gentle, quiet, loving, gray-blue haired and aproned women who like kittens, puppies, and children. They spread happiness and good, sound advice about while cheerfully dispensing milk and cookies and peanut butter and jelly sandwiches and generous plates of delicious fried chicken and mashed potatoes to children and grandchildren "to get some meat on your bones." Grandma in *The Two-Thousand-Pound Goldfish*, however, is not a stereotype. She is not very kind to her grandchildren, Warren and Weezie, and readers can understand and sympathize with this 60-year-old woman's predicament, although she is not the first grandmother who has been left with her grandchildren to rear, whatever the reasons or circumstances. Because she is not in good health, she seems much older than 60. Her legs are swollen—"legs like balloons" (*Goldfish*, 17) she tells Warren—and when she goes downstairs in her apartment building, she has to take "the steps slowly, one by one, like a child" (*Goldfish*, 37). She never leaves her apartment except on Sundays, when she goes to her daughter Pepper's, and she wears "her best bedroom slippers" (*Goldfish*, 39), not shoes. When the Oglebys have a fire in their apartment, she refuses to go down the stairs: " 'Send the

firemen up when they get here,' she called down the stairs to the depart-
ing tenants. 'But if they carry me down, they have to carry me back
up!' " (*Goldfish*, 79–80).

Her indifference toward and lack of affection for her grandchildren,
especially young Warren, stems from several reasons only hinted at, but
perhaps her attitude comes from her bitterness at having to rear her
grandchildren, from her disappointment in two of her daughters, Saffron
and Ginger, and from how she mistakenly and insensitively perceives
Weezie and Warren's attitude toward her. Late one night, Grandma
finds Warren in the bathroom studying the few postcards he and Weezie
have received over the years from their mother. Seeing Warren pouring
over the postcards, Grandma's "eyes acknowledged his childish stupidity." Clenching his fists, Warren rushes at Grandma as if he could strike
her. She becomes angry, showing not only her own bitterness and disappointment but also her lack of insight into Warren's emotional needs.
Angry and full of resentment, she says, "If this is what my whole life
boils down to—one daughter [Ginger] in Las Vegas I haven't seen in
two years, one [Saffron] who's a wanted criminal, a granddaughter that
thinks she's too smart for me, and a grandson who waits in the bathroom in the middle of the night to strike me—well, if that's what life is,
just go ahead and strike!" (*Goldfish*, 61).

Out of her hurt and disappointment, Grandma denies the existence of
her daughter Saffron, on the run and hiding from the FBI for her part in
subversive activities—putting stink bombs in a hotel ventilating system
during a nuclear conference, exploding pipe bombs at chemical plants,
and throwing Molotov cocktails at executive limousines: " 'Your mother's dead,' his grandmother would say flatly. She would not even allow
her name to be mentioned in the apartment" (*Goldfish*, 25).

Grandma is proud of her daughter Pepper, perhaps for the wrong reasons, but still pleased with her because, as she tells a bus driver on one of
her and Warren's Sunday excursions to Pepper's apartment for lunch,
Pepper one time had a part in a soap opera: "She was on seven episodes
and got killed in a car crash. Burned up. They never found the body"
(*Goldfish*, 38). As proud as Grandma is of Pepper's seven episodes, what
she ironically does not guess is that Pepper's character was dispensable or
perhaps played so poorly that the producer and director had to get her
character out of the soap permanently. Bus drivers and Pepper are the
only people Grandma ever talks to with kindness and enthusiasm: "She
liked them [bus drivers]. No bus driver had ever—in her fifty years of
riding buses—been rude to her" (*Goldfish*, 39).

Grandma, however, is more than a sick, disgruntled, and disappointed old woman. Byars shows her as somewhat eccentric, making her more
human and adding a little humor to her character. At one time
Grandma must have had some fire in her slightly askew imagination
because she named her three daughters for spices: Ginger, Pepper, and
Saffron, Warren and Weezie's mother, known as Saffee, "the only one
who had a nickname" (*Goldfish*, 26).

Perhaps from necessity, Grandma is a slovenly housekeeper, but her
slovenliness gives her an added dimension, making a reader smile, if not
laugh. She believes it "a waste of energy to sweep floors more than once
a month . . . [and doesn't] believe in washing clothes often either"
(*Goldfish*, 36). She buys only "brown towels because they never showed
dirt. 'You never have to wash them unless you want to'" (*Goldfish*, 90).
Apparently, Grandma does not believe in banks or in mattresses as safe
places to keep her money. She hides hers in a carton of frozen green
beans in the freezer section of the refrigerator.

Grandma is a pack rat, euphemistically known as a "collector." She
"never got rid of anything. She was known for her collections—twenty-
three bed pillows [which she sleeps on piled underneath her], seventeen
perfume bottles, eleven miniature lamps." Warren "himself sometimes
felt like part of a disappointingly small collection when she said, 'And this
is Warren, one of my two grandchildren'" (*Goldfish*, 77). After Grandma's
death, Pepper packs her collections away, including "her combs and
brushes, . . . her china señorita doll with the lace mantilla, . . . her plastic
flower arrangements" (*Goldfish*, 121). Whatever good, bad, or flawed
traits Grandma has, she is not a stereotypical grandmother.

The most recent elderly person in the Byars canon is Pop in *Coast to
Coast*, a chronologically related story about 13-year-old Birch's seven-day
flight to California with her grandfather, Pop, in his Piper J-3 Cub. Pop
is not as well delineated as other oldsters Byars has created, but well
enough for readers to know he is facing many of the decisions older people and retirees often face. On the threshold of making major changes in
his life, Pop is resigned to make them. Already confronting the wrenching change caused by his wife's recent death, he decides he will not sell
either his house or his plane, he will not give up Ace, his dog, and he will
not move to a retirement center as he has been planning to do. Through
Pop, Byars may be suggesting that many elderly people may think they
are ready for a retirement home when they are not. After considerable
hesitation, Pop does fly to California in his cub, a 10-year dream. Byars
may be also suggesting that elderly men and women, in their homes of

many years or in retirement homes, may still lead rich and full lives—marching to a different drummer—meeting the challenges of flying a Piper Cub across the country, hiking England's Pennines, learning how to operate a computer, writing an autobiography, or spending a year on a sheep ranch in Australia's outback.

Byars's forte as a novelist for young readers is her creation of believable and consistent young protagonists, who often have sad and serious problems and conflicts, alleviated by Byars's wit and humor. Another forte is her creation of richly varied older men and women that she paints with a few details, but just the right ones to make them real and memorable.[3] From Grandma in *Trouble River* to Pop in *Coast to Coast*, Byars has created a host of unique elderly men and women—never the stereotypes of elderly men and women often found in children's fiction.

Chapter Six

The Achievement of Betsy Byars

Few authors, whether their audience is children or adults, write for a time other than their own, although they hope their writing will last beyond a few years or a generation. Whether Byars's fiction will endure only time and tastes will tell. Thirty years ago no critic of children's fiction would have predicted the sudden decline of the works by the gifted and talented Meindert DeJong, one of the most respected and revered writers for children between 1950 and 1965. DeJong won the 1955 Newbery Medal for *Wheel on the School* (1954); he won the 1969 National Book Award[1] for *Journey from Peppermint Street* (1968); and in 1962 he was the first American writer of children's fiction to win the prestigious international Hans Christian Andersen Award for the body of his work written for children. Yet, today, hardly anyone reads his books, including what is likely his most distinguished book, *The House of Sixty Fathers* (1956), a Newbery Honor book for 1957.

Although Byars has won numerous awards, including the 1971 Newbery Award for *The Summer of the Swans* and the 1981 American Book Award for *The Night Swimmers*, awards are no guarantee of durability or classic status. One of the most popular, most distinguished, and most highly praised American books for children of this century, E. B. White's *Charlotte's Web* (1952), did not win a major award. Paradoxically, the 1953 Newbery Award went to Ann Nolan Clark's *Secret of the Andes* (1952), a book few know about today and even fewer read. Since the book's publication, hardly any American who has gone through an American public or private elementary school not only has heard of but also has read *Charlotte's Web*.

One aspect of Byars's fiction and of a number of other writers of children's fiction is that their subject matter is often topically contemporary, making their work somewhat quickly dated. Although books about World War II are still occasionally published, such as Lois Lowry's *Number the Stars* (1989), the number of books for children about that war published in the decades after its close are hardly known today, despite the quality of writing some of them exhibit, as do Anne Frank's *The Diary of a Young Girl* (1952) and Ann Holm's *North To Freedom* (1965), even in their translations. Although works dealing with contemporary concerns often have universal themes, the currency of their topics or subjects often relegates them to the back shelves or to the remainder bins. They may not hold readers' attention for longer periods because there are always new topics and new books demanding attention, driving out older books. They may not last longer because of economic necessity; no matter how good a book is, if it is not bought, a publishing house cannot afford to keep it on its backlists; and if it is not read, a library cannot keep it on its shelves.

Byars's fiction does have enduring qualities. Byars has often captured the essence and the appeal of children, especially those who suffer unmitigated pain at the hands of ignorant, immature, or uncaring adults or from circumstances that only a malevolent fate seems to bring about and to control or from both. Byars's canon is filled with these kinds of children—Figgy in *After the Goat Man*; Thomas J, Harvey, and Carlie in *The Pinballs*; Warren in *The Two-Thousand-Pound Goldfish*; Anna in *The Glory Girl*, and Sammy in *After the Goat Man*, to name a few. Many of these children are often as memorable as the young David Copperfield and Oliver Twist, both of whom suffer the same kinds of hurt from adults and from a malevolent fate. If a comparison of these young characters in Byars's novels with Copperfield and Twist seems undue praise for Byars's characters, it must be remembered that Dickens wrote for adults and that Byars writes for a much younger audience, imposing constraints Dickens never dreamed of. Even with the constraints imposed by writing for a young audience, Byars's characters are drawn with less bathos than Dickens's young Copperfield, Twist, and other young characters in his canon.

Furthermore, Byars has created a host of ordinary yet memorable young characters who are real and genuine but have not been hurt by adults or circumstances beyond their control. They are normal and typical children elevated to prominence by Byars's uncanny talent for creating ordinary youngsters. Bingo Brown and Junior Blossom are children everyone knows; their scintillating personalities, sometimes quelled by a turn of events but rarely for long, are exuberant, ebullient, charming, and delightful. They bring pleasure and lift the human spirit. Byars has also created a dozen exceptional elderly characters. Few contemporary writers for children have created as many varied older men and woman as Byars has. They run a gamut from the somewhat idealized Grammy in the *Bingo Brown* series to the reclusive Mad Mary in the *Blossom* series.

Byars's stories are filled with the kind of humor only Byars can create—from the pure slapstick that children indulge in to ironically subtle and intellectual humor. Byars's humor rises from ironic situations, from the natures of her characters, and from her own characteristic sense of humor. In one of her most suspenseful stories, *Cracker Jackson*, she introduces humor to lessen the terror and impending tragedy she foreshadows from the first sentence of the book.

Byars is a courageous writer, dealing as she often does with such difficult subjects as child and wife abuse in *Cracker Jackson* and the damage done to children by insensitive, foolish, and self-centered parents in *The Cartoonist* and *The Two-Thousand-Pound Goldfish*. Courageously, Byars satirizes some of America's popular institutions. One of her kindest adult characters, Alma in *Cracker Jackson*, is a satire on our predilection for drinking too deeply from the spring of popular culture, reflected in Alma's naming her daughter for a popular character on a television soap opera and Alma's complete collection of Ken and Barbie dolls, symbols of the forever young, tanned, lithe, handsome, well dressed, and vapid. Alma is not unlike parents who name their children for popular singers and film stars and popular wines and liqueurs. Byars is also courageous in presenting some adults as poor excuses for parents.

Byars has written historical realism, fantasy, and contemporary realism, but obviously her forte is contemporary realism—fiction that deals with the ordinary lives of ordinary middle-class people and the crises of their everyday lives. Without middle classes there would be no realistic fiction, because realism *is* the middle classes. If fiction is not about middle classes it is another genre altogether—romance or naturalism or something else.

A major characteristic of realistic fiction is its generally optimistic tone, not because it has satisfying endings but because realistic fiction lifts the human spirit, helps it to prevail and endure, to use Faulkner's phrasing in his Nobel Prize acceptance speech. Despite their being emotionally and sometimes physically abused, these children that frequent Byars's fiction come out on top with hope that they, too, can prevail and endure.

Byars is not a didactic writer, but in many of her novels her depictions of confused, uncaring, unloving, and indifferent parents contrasted with kind, loving, and caring parents are exempla without texts for children, who will someday perhaps be parents themselves. This graphic contrast is not missed by young readers; they will recognize the differences, and their recognition will help them to be kinder, wiser, and maturer adults and parents.

While many of Byars's minor characters and a few of her major characters are flat and static, her most unforgettable characters are boys and girls who grow and change for the better. Many of these characters experience an epiphany, recognize a moment of truth, discover a truth about themselves and the human condition that makes them better at the end of a story than they were at the beginning. Having read Byars's novels, young people will be better able to understand and recognize their own moments of epiphany, moments of truth—those truths that are steps toward the kind of maturity that all thoughtful people, including adults, are striving for all their lives.

If Byars's stories do not survive in print for another generation, the goodness of her fiction will live in the descendants of her young readers of today. This is the efficacy of literary art, and Byars's art is efficacious.

Notes and References

Chapter One

1. *The Moon and I* (New York: Messner, 1991), 41–42; hereafter cited in text as *Moon*.
2. Interviews with Betsy Byars, 7 February 1989 and at various times by telephone; hereafter cited in text as *Int*.
3. "Betsy Byars," in *Something about the Author, Autobiography Series*, ed. Adele Sarkissian (Detroit: Gale Research, 1988), 1:56; hereafter cited in text as *Author*.
4. *Cracker Jackson* (New York: Viking, 1985), 35; hereafter cited in text as *Cracker*.
5. "So many of these [writers of fantasy, Kipling, Grahame, Potter, Anderson, White, etc.] suffered childhood unhappiness that it might almost appear a prerequisite of creativity—an intense unhappiness that made the writer unusually sensitive to his own existence and to the world about him and forced him into a vivid inner life" (Eleanor Cameron, *The Green and Burning Tree* [Boston: Little Brown, 1969], 6–7). Some of the children in Byars's stories support Cameron's hypothesis. The protagonists of *The TV Kid, The Cartoonist*, and *The Two-Thousand-Pound Goldfish* are unhappy and escape into lives of their own creations.
6. Margaret Mazurkiewicz and Jean W. Ross, "Byars, Betsy (Cromer)," in *Contemporary Authors*, New Revised Series, vol. 18, ed. Linda Metzger and Deborah A. Straub (Detroit: Gale Research, 1986), 74; hereafter cited in text.
7. For many centuries in all parts of the world, wild boars have been and are still hunted for sport, but only young boars are slaughtered and eaten. In the United States, however, eating wild boar meat is discouraged by state and federal health agencies, not only because of its unpalatability but because of diseases the boars carry. Only domestically raised barrows and sows are slaughtered and sold commercially in the United States today. This information comes from Dr. George Skelly, professor of applied animal science and Dr. John Diehl, professor of animal and swine endocrinology, at Clemson University.
8. "Writing for Children," *Signal* 37 (1982): 5.

Chapter Two

1. *The Midnight Fox* (New York: Viking, 1968), 45; hereafter cited in text as *Fox*.
2. *The Summer of the Swans* (New York: Viking, 1970) 13; hereafter cited in text as *Swans*.

3. Elizabeth Segel, "Betsy Byars," in *Dictionary of Literary Biography: American Writers for Children since 1960: Fiction*, vol. 52, ed. Glenn E. Estes (Detroit: Gale Research, 1986), 56; hereafter cited in text.

4. *The House of Wings* (New York: Viking, 1972), 48; hereafter cited in text as *Wings*.

5. *The 18th Emergency* (New York: Viking, 1973), 9; hereafter cited in text as *18th*.

6. David Rees, "Little Bit of Ivory—Betsy Byars," *Painted Desert, Green Shade* (Boston: Horn Book, 1984), 35; hereafter cited in text.

7. *After the Goat Man* (New York: Viking, 1974), 23–24; hereafter cited in text as *Goat*.

8. Giving inappropriate names to children, as the twins' father gives them, is grist for Byars's satire in several instances throughout her canon.

9. With Carlie's hitting her stepfather with a double boiler, Byars instantly reveals a facet of Carlie's character—she has spirit.

10. *The Pinballs* (New York: Harper, 1976), 5; hereafter cited in text as *Pinballs*.

11. Elizabeth Yates has a true story for young readers about a dog helping young, hospitalized convalescents in *Skeezer, a Dog with a Mission* (New York: Harvey House, 1973).

12. *The Night Swimmers* won the American Book Award for 1981, not the National Book Award, as some think; the National Book Award was discontinued in 1979, replaced by the American Book Award.

13. *The Night Swimmers* (New York: Delacorte, 1980), 6; hereafter cited in text as *Swimmers*.

14. *The Two-Thousand-Pound Goldfish* (New York: Harper, 1982), 51–52; hereafter cited in text as *Goldfish*.

15. Katherine Paterson, *The Great Gilly Hopkins* (New York: Avon, 1979), 147.

Chapter Three

1. Quoted in Cleanth Brooks, R. W. B. Lewis, and Robert Penn Warren, eds., "Tale and Character," in *American Literature: The Makers and the Making*, vol. 1 (New York: St. Martin's, 1973), 1090; hereafter cited in text.

2. *The Not-Just-Anybody Family* (New York: Delacorte, 1986), 1; hereafter cited in text as *Family*.

3. *The Blossoms Meet the Vulture Lady* (New York: Delacorte, 1986), 69–71; hereafter cited in text as *Lady*.

4. Allen F. Stein and Thomas N. Walters, Introduction to *The Southern Experience in Short Fiction* (Glenview, Ill.: Scott Foresman, 1971), 4.

5. On the importance of land to southerners, see Stein and Walters, Introduction to *The Southern Experience in Short Fiction*, 2, and Alan Tate, "The Profession of Letters in the South," in *Essays of Four Decades* (Chicago: Swallow, 1968), 521.

6. On the importance of community in the South, see Louis D. Rubin, Jr., and C. Hugh Holman, eds., "Thematic Problems in Southern Literature," *Southern Literature Study: Problems and Possibilities* (Chapel Hill: University of North Carolina Press, 1975), 199–222, and Louis D. Rubin, Jr., *The Faraway Country* (Seattle: University of Washington Press, 1963), 3–20.

7. Johanna Spyri's *Heidi* (English translation, 1884), Frances Hodgson Burnett's *Little Lord Fauntleroy* (1886), and Kate Douglas Wiggin's *Rebecca of Sunnybrook Farm* (1902) are three examples among several in which a child brings an older person back to a sense of community.

8. *The Burning Questions of Bingo Brown* (New York: Viking, 1988), 4–5; hereafter cited in text as *Questions*.

9. *Bingo Brown and the Language of Love* (New York: Viking, 1989), 72; hereafter cited in text as *Language*.

10. *Bingo Brown, Gypsy Lover* (New York: Viking, 1990), 4–5; hereafter cited in text as *Gypsy*.

11. *Bingo Brown's Guide to Romance* (New York: Viking, 1992), 5; hereafter cited in text as *Romance*.

12. Later in *Bingo Brown, Gypsy Lover* (62) Bingo recalls this episode in similar detail.

13. In her canon Byars has often picked up on this and other contemporary nuances that indicate changes in American mores since the 1960s.

Chapter Four

1. *The Cartoonist* (New York: Viking, 1978), 27; hereafter cited in text as *Cartoonist*.

2. *McMummy* (New York: Viking, 1991), 13; hereafter cited in text as *Mummy*.

3. Eudora Welty, *The Ponder Heart* (San Diego: Harvest/Harcourt, 1985), 116.

4. *The Glory Girl* (New York: Viking, 1983), 31; hereafter cited in text as *Glory*.

5. Mary Magdalen was portrayed in sculpture as well. Donatello's (1386?–1466) life-sized sculpture depicts her weeping, the epitome of sorrow.

Chapter Five

1. *Good-bye, Chicken Little* (New York: Harper, 1979), 46; hereafter cited in text as *Chicken*.

2. *Trouble River* (New York: Viking, 1969), 53.

3. Byars has two other memorable elderly characters: Ira Gryshevich in *After the Goat Man*, discussed in Chapter 2, and Mad Mary Campbell in the *Blossom* series, discussed in Chapter 3.

Chapter Six

1. The National Book Award was discontinued in 1979, replaced by the American Book Award, beginning in 1980. A few sources mistakenly say that Byars won the National Book Award for *The Night Swimmers*.

Selected Bibliography

PRIMARY WORKS

Books

After the Goat Man. New York: Viking, 1974.
The Animal, the Vegetable, and John D Jones. New York: Delacorte, 1982.
Beans on the Roof. New York: Delacorte, 1988.
Bingo Brown and the Language of Love. New York: Viking, 1989.
Bingo Brown, Gypsy Lover. New York: Viking, 1990.
Bingo Brown's Guide to Romance. New York: Viking, 1992.
A Blossom Promise. New York: Delacorte, 1987.
The Blossoms and the Green Phantom. New York: Delacorte, 1987.
The Blossoms Meet the Vulture Lady. New York: Delacorte, 1986.
The Burning Questions of Bingo Brown. New York: Viking, 1988.
The Cartoonist. New York: Viking, 1978.
Clementine. Boston: Houghton Mifflin, 1962.
Coast to Coast. New York: Delacorte, 1992.
The Computer Nut. New York: Viking, 1984.
Cracker Jackson. New York: Viking, 1985.
The Cybil War. New York: Viking, 1981.
The Dancing Camel. New York: Viking, 1965.
The 18th Emergency. New York: Viking, 1973.
The Glory Girl. New York: Viking, 1983.
Go and Hush the Baby. New York: Viking, 1971.
The Golly Sisters Go West. New York: Harper, 1985.
The Golly Sisters Ride Again. New York: HarperCollins, 1994.
Good-bye, Chicken Little. New York: Harper, 1979.
The Groober. New York: Harper, 1967.
Hooray for the Golly Sisters! New York: Harper, 1990.
The House of Wings. New York: Viking, 1972.
The Lace Snail. New York: Viking, 1975.
McMummy. New York: Viking, 1983.
The Midnight Fox. New York: Viking, 1968.
The Moon and I. New York: Messner, 1991
The Night Swimmers. New York: Delacorte, 1980.
The Not-Just-Anybody Family. New York: Delacorte, 1986.
The Pinballs. New York: Harper, 1977.
Rama, the Gypsy Cat. New York: Viking, 1966.

The Seven Treasure Hunts. New York: Harper/Collins, 1991.
The Summer of the Swans. New York: Viking, 1970.
Trouble River. New York: Viking, 1968.
The TV Kid. New York: Viking, 1976.
The Two-Thousand-Pound Goldfish. New York: Harper, 1982.
Wanted . . . Mud Blossom. New York: Delacorte, 1991.
The Winged Colt of Casa Mia. New York: Viking, 1973.

Articles and Essays

"Afterword." *Five Little Peppers and How They Grew*, by Margaret Sidney. New York: Dell, 1985. On the appeal of the novel 100 years after its first publication in 1880.

"Beginnings, 'Human Things,' and the Magic Moment." *Proceedings of the Eighth Annual Conference of the Children's Literature Association, University of Minnesota, March 1981*, edited by Priscilla A. Ord. Boston: Children's Literature Association, 1982. Discusses origins of several novels.

"Betsy Byars." In *Something about the Author, Autobiography Series*, edited by Adele Sarkissian. Vol. 1. Detroit: Gale Research, 1986. An account of Byars's life through 1985.

"Leo Edwards and the Secret and Mysterious Order of the Freckled Goldfish." *Horn Book* 61 (September–October 1985): 533–35. On Byars's childhood reading of Leo Edwards's series books and their possible influence on her writing.

"Newbery Award Acceptance." In *New Newbery and Caldecott Medal Books, 1966–1975*, edited by Lee Kingman. Boston: Horn Book, 1975. On winning the award and a tongue-in-cheek account of the four stages of writing a book.

"Writing for Children." *Signal* 37 (January 1982): 3–10. On writing and the geneses of several books.

SECONDARY WORKS

Chambers, Aidan. "Letter from England: Arrows—All Pointing Upward." *Horn Book* 54 (December 1978): 680–84. Chambers finds few flaws in Byars's fiction and praises its overall quality.

Hansen, I. V. "A Decade of Betsy Byars' Boys." *Children's Literature in Education* 15 (Spring 1984): 3–11. Praises Byars's portraits of young boys with emphasis on Mouse in *The 18th Emergency* and Simon in *The Cybil War*.

Rees, David. "Little Bit of Ivory—Betsy Byars." In *Painted Desert, Green Shade*. Boston: Horn Book, 1984. Perhaps the best critical analysis of Byars's work to date, praising her originality, her "succinct prose style with terse, vivid perceptions and ironical observations of life."

Robertson, Ina. "Profile: Betsy Byars—Writer for Today's Child." *Language Arts* 57 (March 1980): 328–34. Traces Byars's increasing confidence in her writing through 1979.

Segel, Elizabeth. "Betsy Byars: An Interview." *Children's Literature in Education* 31 (Winter 1982): 171–79. A discussion of some elements in Byars's life and writing.

———. "Betsy Byars." In *Dictionary of Literary Biography: American Writers for Children since 1960: Fiction*, Vol. 52, edited by Glenn E. Estes, 52–66. Detroit: Gale Research, 1986. Good, brief evaluations of Byars's books published through 1985.

Watson, Ken. "The Art of Betsy Byars." *Orana* 16 (February 1980): 3–5. Traces Byars's developing skills and talents in style and plot.

Manuscripts and Related Materials

Clemson University has first editions, foreign-language editions, manuscripts, galleys, videos, and related materials given by Byars. Clemson University Libraries Special Collections, P.O. Box 343001, Clemson, SC 29634-3001.

Index

The Author

A native Texan, Malcolm Usrey is professor emeritus of English at Clemson University. He holds a B.A. from Abilene Christian University and an M.A. and Ph.D. from Texas Technological University. He held various offices in the Children's Literature Association and served as president in 1985–86. From 1972 through 1990 he began and directed the annual Children's Literature Symposia at Clemson, where he taught English and children's literature for 29 years. He has published articles on children's literature in various journals, and from 1981 until his retirement he served as editor of Clemson University's "Books for Children," a weekly review service syndicated in the Southeast.

The Editor

Ruth K. MacDonald is associate dean of Bay Path College. She received her B.A. and M.A. in English from the University of Connecticut, her Ph.D. in English from Rutgers University, and her M.B.A. from the University of Texas at El Paso. To Twayne's United States and English Authors series she has contributed the volumes on Louisa May Alcott, Beatrix Potter, and Dr. Seuss. She is also the author of *Literature for Children in England and America, 1646–1774* (1982).